ISBN 978-0-331-38548-9
PIBN 11115997

Historic, archived document

Do not assume content reflects current
scientific knowledge, policies, or practices.

FOREIGN CROPS AND MARKETS.

ISSUED WEEKLY BY THE BUREAU OF AGRICULTURAL ECONOMICS,
UNITED STATES DEPARTMENT OF AGRICULTURE, WASHINGTON, D. C.

VOLUME 12   MAY 17, 1926   NO. 20

Feature of issue: VEGETABLE OILS AND OIL SEEDS

BULGARIA WHEAT AREA EQUAL TO LAST YEAR, CORN DECREASED.

The wheat area of Bulgaria, including both winter and spring crops, is estimated at 2,535,000 acres, according to a cable from the International Institute of Agriculture. This is about equal to the 2,537,000 acres reported harvested for 1924-25. Detailed figures of winter and spring acreage are not reported. Unless there was a downward revision of winter wheat acreage, this estimate indicates a material decrease in spring wheat acreage. The fall sown area as previously reported was 2,503,000 acres compared with 2,384,000 last year, an increase of 5.0 per cent.

Rye acreage is placed at 427,000 acres compared with 453,000 last year, corn 1,463,000 acres compared with 1,531,000, barley 534,000 acres compared with 544,000 and oats 400,000 compared with 354,000.

- - - - - - - - - -

BRITISH MARKETS RECOVERING FROM STRIKE

Improved market conditions have followed the official declaration ending the British general strike, according to cabled advices as of May 15 from E. A. Foley, American Agricultural Commissioner at London. Inactivity still prevails at the docks, but there are indications that dockers and transport workers will return to work soon. The railways have already resumed operation. Danish hog killings for export to Great Britain have also been resumed. No material decrease is expected in the future demand for the American agricultural products usually sent to Great Britain, with the possible exception of raw cotton. Sugar prices have been fixed at 6.57 cents per pound in London and 7.07 cents elsewhere. See page 641.

THE SITUATION IN VEGETABLE OILS

Figures for 1925 indicate a potential world supply of vegetable oils greater than that of 1924. Trade figures for the last five years indicate a tendency toward heavier consumption in importing countries. Prices since January 1925 have declined for most vegetable oils. Copra and coconut oil, rapeseed and rapeseed oil and olives and olive oil are the notable exceptions to the downward movement in prices. See pages 639 and 647.

CROP PROSPECTS
CEREAL CROPS
Spring Sowings

Weather conditions in Canada have been favorable for the sowing of
spring crops and seeding is well in advance of last year. The United States
Weather Bureau reports rainfall in the Prairie Provinces which should improve
the growing crops. Previous reports had mentioned a growing need of rain.
Southern Alberta and southwestern Saskatchewan got one good rain and southeastern Saskatchewan two rains during the week of May 12. In the rest of the
Prairie Provinces, good to heavy rains were reported. The temperature was
above normal in all the Prairie region and in Manitoba a maximum above 80°
was reported.

Winter Crops

Reports from Europe are on the whole favorable. Cabled reports of
conditions of winter wheat and rye about the first of May are above average
and better than last year for Germany and the Netherlands. For wheat this
condition holds good for Poland, Austria and Belgium also. In Austria
the rye condition, although above average, was poorer than last year. In
Italy the crop condition is generally good in the northern section but
cooler weather is wanted in the southern part. The condition of the winter
cereal crops in the southeastern region of Russia and the Volga region was
satisfactory on April 20, the International Institute reports, while in the
Ukraine the condition on April 15, although slightly below average was
better than last year. Trade reports comment on a backward season in
Russia. The Russian Information Bureau states that improved varieties of
seeds are being used this spring, which, it is claimed, will increase the
yield 2 to 5 1/2 bushels per acre.

BREAD GRAINS: Acreage of winter sowings, average 1909-13, annual 1924-1926

Crop and country	Average 1909-13 a/	1924	1925	1926 Preliminary	Per cent 1926 is of 1925
WHEAT	1,000 acres	1,000 acres	1,000 acres	1,000 acres	Per cent
Total, 11 countries b/c/ ......:	60,077	65,397	67,743	64,732	95.6
Canada, harvested area.........:	1,053	774	794	753	94.8
United States, harvested area..:	28,382	35,489	31,269	37,085	118.6
Luxemburg, revised.............:	27	22	22	25	113.6
Rumania, revised...............:	8,183	6,632	7,236	7,072	97.7
Morocco, " ....:	1,700	2,461	2,545	2,684	105.5
Algeria, " ....:	3,521	3,492	3,407	3,562	104.5
Total, 17 countries...........:	102,943	114,267	112,016	115,913	103.5

Continued -

C R O P   P R O S P E C T S,   C O N T ' D

BREAD GRAINS: Acreage of winter sowings, average 1909-13, annual 1924-1926, cont'd.

Crop and country	Average 1909-13 a/	1924	1925	1926 Preliminary	Per cent 1926 is of 1925
RYE d/					
Total, 10 countries e/.........	24,280	19,566	20,806	20,639	99.2
Canada, revised...............	117	891	703	653	92.9
United States, revised.........	2,235	4,019	4,088	3,565	87.2
Luxemburg....................	26	16	17	15	88.2
Total, 13 countries...........	26,659	24,492	25,614	24,872	97.1

a/ Where changes in boundaries have occurred as a result of the world war, estimates have been adjusted to correspond with the area within the post-war boundaries.   b/ Estimates for earlier years given for comparison refer to winter acreage only where comparable statistics of winter seedings are available, in some of the minor producing countries where most of the crop is winter wheat and where abandonment is of little significance estimates of earlier year given for comparison are the final estimates of the total crop.   c/ Includes England and Wales, France, Italy, Czechoslovakia, Bulgaria, Poland, Lithuania, Finland, Belgium, Tunis and India.   d/ Estimates of earlier years for comparisons are final estimates of the total winter and spring area harvested.   e/ Includes France, Czechoslovakia, Bulgaria, Rumania, Poland, Lithuania, Latvia, Finland, Italy and Belgium.

The total winter and spring acreage for the 1926 wheat crop in Czechoslovakia is reported as 1,541,000 acres according to a cable from the International Institute of Agriculture. This is an increase of 15,000 acres over last year's total of 1,526,000. This increase is partly offset by the decrease of 10,000 acres under rye which is reported at 2,080,000 acres compared with 2,090,000 last year. Other grains show slight increases, barley 1,735,000 acres against 1,714,000 last year, oats 2,093,000 against 2,068,000 and corn 390,000 against 387,000 last year.

<u>Corn</u>

The corn area of Bulgaria is reported at 1,463,000 acres compared with 1,531,000 acres in 1925. The 1925-26 corn crop in the Union of South Africa is estimated at 41,061,000 bushels compared with 73,215,000 bushels for 1924-25 and 51,000,000 bushels the average for the five years 1920-24. Exports during the first 10 months of 1925, the heavy export season amounted to 26,000,000 bush

CEREAL CROPS: Production 1924 and 1925

Crop and country	1924	1925	Per cent 1925 is of 1924
WHEAT	1,000 bushels	1,000 bushels	Per cent
Total, 41 countries..............	2,706,294	2,969,021	109.7
India, revised..................	360,640	321,953	89.3
Total, 42 countries..............	3,066,934	3,290,934	107.3
Estimated world total excluding Russia.......................	3,098,000		

Continued -

C R O P   P R O S P E C T S,   C O N T ' D
- - - - - -

CEREAL CROPS: Production 1924 and 1925, cont'd

Crop and Country	1924	1925	Per cent 1925 is of 1924
RYE	1,000 bushels	1,000 bushels	Per cent
Total, 27 countries ....:	728,282	1,001,992	137.6
Argentina, revised ....:	1,457	4,733	324.8
Total, 28 countries ....:	729,739	1,006,725	138.0
Estimated world total excluding			
Russia ....:	743,000		
BARLEY			
Total, 37 countries ....:	1,050,192	1,239,336	118.0
Argentina, revised ....:	6,974	17,055	244.6
Total, 38 countries ....:	1,057,166	1,256,391	118.8
Estimated world total excluding			
Russia........................:	1,207,000		
OATS			
Total, 35 countries ....:	3,538,070	3,790,176	107.1
Argentina, revised ....:	53,457	80,433	150.5
Total, 36 countries ....:	3,591,527	3,870,609	107.8
Estimated world total excluding			
Russia ....:	3,675,000		
CORN			
Total, 19 countries ....:	2,939,649	3,532,315	120.2
Argentina ....:	186,301	279,000	149.8
Union of South Africa ....:	73,214	41,051	56.1
Total, 21 countries ....:	3,199,164	3,852,376	120.4
Estimated world total excluding			
Russia ....:	3,213,000		

- - - - - -

SUGAR

     The German Sugar Association estimates the acreage sown to sugarbeets in Germany at 905,000 acres, or 1.2 per cent below their estimate for last year's acreage, according to a cable of May 12 from the International Institute at Rome.

     Reports received to date from the International Institute, including German Czechoslovakia, Hungary and Russia, indicate an increase of 8 per cent over last year in the total sugar beet area for those countries, which included about 60 per cent of the total European sugar beet acreage harvested in 1925. The figures reported by the International Institute are estimates made by the Sugar Association of the various countries and are as follows:

CROP PROSPECTS, CONT'D

SUGAR BEETS: Area in specified European Countries, 1925 and 1926

Country	1925	1926	Per cent 1926 is of 1925
	Acres	Acres	Per cent
rmany................:	916,000	905,000	98.8
echoslovakia..........:	770,000	648,000	84.2
ngary................:	164,200	153,700	96.7
ssia.................:	1,167,800	1,558,000	133.4
tal.................:	3,018,000	3,269,700	108.3
therlands............:	163,600		90.0 to 95.0

The total European sugar beet acreage as estimated by Dr. Gustav Mikusch Vienna places the 1926 beet sowings at 5,349,000 acres or 6.3 per cent above s corresponding estimate for 1925, according to a cable from Commissioner Haas Vienna. This total is the same as that of F. O. Licht although estimates for e individual countries vary.

The 1926 cane sugar crop of Australia will probably show a considerable crease from last year's production of 581,000 short tons, according to a trade per of May 1. The rainy season has been much delayed in most districts of eensland and as a result the cane growth has been retarded. Australia's inding season usually begins in May.

SUGAR: Production of cane and beet sugar in countries reporting for 1925-26

Country	1924-25	1925-26	Per cent 1925-26 is of 1924-25
BEET SUGAR	Short tons	Short tons	Per cent
oduction, 14 countries previously reported and unrevised............:	6,826,462	6,709,822	98.3
vised estimates received –			
England......................:	29,745	63,815	214.5
Netherlands..................:	351,977	329,608	93.6
Belgium......................:	438,362	360,736	82.3
Spain........................:	277,823	267,624	96.3
Italy........................:	460,715	169,360	36.8
Switzerland..................:	6,614	7,163	108.3
Austria......................:	82,800	86,200	104.1
Russia.......................:	501,977	1,083,340	215.8
timated world total beet sugar a/:	8,976,475	9,077,670	101.1

Continued –

CROP PROSPECTS, CONT'D

CEREAL CROPS: Production 1924 and 1925, cont'd

Crop and Country	1924	1925	Per cent 19 is of 192
RYE	:1,000 bushels	:1,000 bushels	Per cent
Total, 27 countries ....:	728,282	1,001,992	. 137.6
Argentina, revised ....:	1,457	4,733	324.8
Total, 28 countries ....:	729,739	1,006,725	138.0
Estimated world total excluding :			
Russia ....:	743,000		
BARLEY			
Total, 37 countries ....:	1,050,192	1,239,336	118.0
Argentina, revised ....:	6,974	17,055	244.6
Total, 38 countries ....:	1,057,166	1,256,391	118.8
Estimated world total excluding :			
Russia........................:	1,207,000		
OATS			
Total, 35 countries ....:	3,538,070	3,790,176	107.1
Argentina, revised ....:	53,457	80,433	150.5
Total, 36 countries ....:	3,591,527	3,870,609	107.8
Estimated world total excluding :			
Russia ....:	3,675,000		
CORN			
Total, 19 countries ....:	2,939,649	3,532,315	120.2
Argentina ....:	186,301	279,000	149.8
Union of South Africa ....:	73,214	41,051	56.1
Total, 21 countries ....:	3,199,164	3,852,376	120.4
Estimated world total excluding :			
Russia ....:	3,213,000		

- - - - - -

SUGAR

The German Sugar Association estimates the acreage sown to sugarbeets Germany at 905,000. acres, or 1.2 per cent below their estimate for last year acreage, according to a cable of May 12 from the International Institute at Rome.

Reports received to date from the International Institute, including G Czechoslovakia, Hungary and Russia, indicate an increase of 8 per cent over 1 year in the total sugar beet area for those countries, which included about 6 cent of. the total European sugar beet acreage harvested in.1925. The figures reported by the International Institute are estimares made by the Sugar Assoc of the various countries and are as follows:

CROP PROSPECTS, CONT'D

SUGAR BEETS: Area in specified European Countries, 1925 and 1926

Country	1925	1926	Per cent 1926 is of 1925
	Acres	Acres	Per cent
Germany....................	916,000	905,000	98.8
Czechoslovakia.............	770,000	648,000	84.2
Hungary....................	164,200	153,700	96.7
Russia.....................	1,167,800	1,558,000	133.4
Total.....................	3,018,000	3,269,700	108.3
Netherlands................	163,600		90.0 to 95.0

The total European sugar beet acreage as estimated by Dr. Gustav Mikusch of Vienna places the 1926 beet sowings at 5,349,000 acres or 6.3 per cent above his corresponding estimate for 1925, according to a cable from Commissioner Haas at Vienna. This total is the same as that of F. O. Licht although estimates for the individual countries vary.

The 1926 cane sugar crop of Australia will probably show a considerable decrease from last year's production of 581,000 short tons, according to a trade paper of May 1. The rainy season has been much delayed in most districts of Queensland and as a result the cane growth has been retarded. Australia's grinding season usually begins in May.

SUGAR: Production of cane and beet sugar in countries reporting for 1925-26

Country	1924-25	1925-26	Per cent 1925-26 is of 1924-25
BEET SUGAR	Short tons	Short tons	Per cent
Production, 14 countries previously reported and unrevised............	6,826,462	6,709,822	98.3
Revised estimates received —			
England........................	29,745	63,815	214.5
Netherlands....................	351,977	329,808	93.6
Belgium........................	438,362	360,736	82.3
Spain..........................	277,823	267,624	96.3
Italy..........................	460,715	169,360	36.8
Switzerland....................	6,614	7,163	108.3
Austria........................	82,300	86,200	104.1
Russia.........................	501,977	1,083,740	215.8
Estimated world total beet sugar a/:	8,976,475	9,077,670	101.1

Continued —

C R O P   P R O S P E C T S,   C O N T ' D

SUGAR, CONT'D

. SUGAR: Production of cane and beet sugar in countries reporting for 1925-26, cont'd

Country	1924-25	1925-26	Per cent 1925-26 is of 1924-25
CANE SUGAR	Short tons	Short tons	Per cent
Production, 28 countries previously reported and unrevised............	8,099,225	8,618,217	106.4
Revised estimates received —			
Porto Rico	630,000	593,000	89.8
Cuba	5,812,068	b/ 5,330,046	91.7
Java.........................	2,202,295	2,335,293	115.1
Egypt.......................	82,203	82,672	100.6
Reunion.....................	58,666	61,000	104.0
Australia...................	489,592	581,299	118.7
Total, 34 countries reporting.......	17,404,049	17,801,527	102.3
Estimated world total cane sugar....	17,623,000	18,022,000	102.3

Official sources, International Institute of Agriculture, Estimates of Sugar Associations and Commercial Estimates.
a/ Exclusive of production in minor producing countries for which no data are available. b/ Revised in accordance with the Cuban Crop Reduction Law which provides for a reduction of 10 per cent of the average of the three most reliable production estimates.

- - - - - -

COTTON

The damage from insects in Colombia previously reported is now estimated to be 75 per cent of the crop, according to Consul Schrare at Cartagena.

The steady development of cotton-growing in Iraq shows every prospect of continuing during 1926, according to the London Times for April 21. Planting at the time of writing was in full swing, and the sales of seed had already exceeded those of 1925. It is expected that nearly 1,000 acres will be planted near Mosul, but the completion of the railway is necessary before this area can be fully developed. The excellent results obtained by pump irrigation are encouraging the development of this type of cultivation, which enables the farmers to plant well-drained land.

In Anglo-Egyptian Sudan, of the revised production estimate of 101,000 bales, for 1925-26, 60,000 were picked before the end of February and nearly 70 per cent of the total production was grown on the Gezira plain, reports the International Institute of Agriculture. In Egypt the weather was favorable during April, according to a cablegram from the Institute.

C R O P P R O S P E C T S, C O N T ' D
- - - - - - -

COTTON, CONT'D

COTTON: Area and production 1924-25 and 1925-26

Country	1924-25	1925-26	Per cent 1925-26 is of 1924-25
ARMA	:1,000 acres	: 1,000 acres	Per cent
Regions previously reporting and unchanged................... :	73,681	80,167	108.8
Syria............................ :	56	97	173.2
Total above regions.............. :	73,737	80,264	108.8
Estimated world total............ :	79,500		
PRODUCTION	:1,000 bales	: 1,000 bales	Per cent
Regions previously reporting and unchanged..................... :	23,673	26,575	112.2
Paraguay......................... :	12	10	83.3
Syria............................ :	21	14	66.7
Union of South Africa............ :	16	25	156.2
Total above regions.............. :	23,722	26,624	112.2
Estimated world total............ :	24,800	27,800	112.1

- - - - - - - -

RICE

The 1925 rice crop of Indo-China is estimated at 7,841,250,000 pounds of cleaned rice compared with 7,858,942,000 pounds in 1924, according to the estimate just received from the International Institute of Agriculture at Rome. This compares favorable with the 1923 crop, which was estimated at 7,212,580,000 pounds and is nearly equal to the large crop of 1922 which totalled 7,893,012,000 pounds.

- - - - - - - -

OILSEEDS

FIRST ESTIMATES OF FLAX SOWINGS FOR 1926: The area sown to flax in Belgium for the 1926 season is estimated at 58,000 acres or the same as that of 1925, according to a cable from the International Institute of Agriculture at Rome. Sowing was aided by fine, dry weather up to the first of April.

In Italy flax sowings are equal to those of 1925 or 49,400 acres. In Morocco a decrease is expected, only 49,400 acres are reported as compared with 55,200 last year. The condition of the crop in Morocco on April 1 was good and promised a yield per acre equivalent to the average yield of the last ten years, according to the International Institute of Agriculture.

L I V E S T O C K,   M E A T   A N D   W O O L   N E W S

Cattle and beef

INCREASED SLAUGHTERING OF CATTLE AND SWINE IN GERMANY: Cattle and swine slaughtering at the 36 most important slaughter points in Germany continue to be high and show an increase over last year. The number of cattle and calves killed during the first 3 months of 1926 was 514,642 or an increase of 5 per cent for the same period of 1924 while hog slaughterings for the first three months of 1926 numbered 837,940 an increase of 10 per cent. Sheep killings, on the other hand, decreased 9 per cent to 218,902. An unusually large number of sheep were butchered in Germany last year. See page 686 for details.

Hogs and pork

GERMAN PORK PRICES STIFFEN: Hog prices at Berlin and lard at Hamburg both appreciated somewhat during the week of May 12, according to W. A. Schoenfeld, American Agricultural Commissioner at Berlin. Hog receipts were heavier. See page 687.

BACON PIG PRODUCTION IN NEW ZEALAND: Pig raising as a side-line to the dairy industry in New Zealand is likely to become a primary industry should English importers of frozen pigs for bacon curing continue their favorable reception of shipments, states Vice Consul Hudson at Wellington, New Zealand. Regularity of supply appears to be the principal problem. In the Fielding District of the North Island a decisive step has been taken in the direction of helping to establish an export trade in the bacon industry by a co-operative organization known as the North Island Dairy Companies, Pig Co-operation. In addition to supplies from that District, the co-operative gets supplies from other adjoining territory. The works where the pigs have been killed have been approved by the Meat Board supervisor and a London buyer, both of whom have expressed satisfaction at the standard of work done. The required weight of pigs to be sold locally in 150 pounds and those for export are fed up to 180 pounds.

Sheep and wool

SEASONAL OUTLOOK IN AUSTRALIA IMPROVED BY RAIN: Recent rains have improved Australia's pastoral situation considerably. The rain means an increase in the wool clip in New South Wales as there will be more sheep to shear and the rain has come at the right time to benefit the clip in the best wool growing months of the year, April to September. It is expected now that by next summer (December, January, February) there will be very large numbers of fat sheep in the country, and that the mutton export will be heavy, states Country Life and Stock and Station Journal of March 30, 1926. Another big lambing is anticipated this year which means that New South Wales will be heavily stocked in sheep and it will be necessary to export considerable numbers. Large numbers of sheep are expected at Homebush Fat Stock Markets, New South Wales after the shearing. Against this probable increase in the New South Wales clip there is to be offset a certain decrease in the wool clip of Queensland. In that State sheep losses have been very heavy and in some districts the losses are still going on.

F R U I T ,   V E G E T A B L E S   A N D   N U T S

LARGE MEDITERRANEAN ALMOND CROP INDICATED: All Mediterranean almond
producing districts are now safe from frost and indications point to a large
crop, according to a cable to the Department of Agriculture from Agricultural
Commissioner Foley at London. The fruit has been developing satisfactorily
in all districts, with no serious frost damage anywhere, notwithstanding some
reports to the contrary. The only adverse reports so far received - cables
from the International Institute of Agriculture and from Consul Nathan at
Palermo - indicate that hot winds did some damage in Sicily during the last
week in April, but no details have yet arrived. Mr. Foley states that some
damage from cold fogs causing fruit to drop may be expected in the Bari section
until around May 15, but prospects, nevertheless, are that the crop in that
region will be large, unless unforseen developments occur.

Prices of almonds, both for prompt and future delivery, have dropped
off sharply in all sections of the basin as a result of the favorable crop
outlook, and very little business is at present being done as a result. Stocks
on hand are not large but are probably somewhat above what previous reports
have indicated. The carryover in Spain at the end of March was estimated at
approximately 20 per cent of last year's crop, although in some markets, particularly Malaga, supplies were low. Sicilian stocks about the same time were
variously estimated at from 10,000 to 25,000 bales of 220 pounds, with a
figure of 15,000 to 20,000 bales most commonly reported. Bari stocks were
estimated at from 30,000 to 40,000 bags of 220 pounds each.

- - - - - - - - -

THE WORLD VEGETABLE OILS AND OILSEEDS SITUATION

An indicated increase in potential supply of vegetable oils is the
outstanding feature of the world situation in those commodities for the
period January 1, 1925 to April 30, 1926. Other leading factors noticeable
over the same period are: A tendency toward heavier world consumption of
those products, and a general downward movement in prices.

The potential production of edible oils for 1925 is indicated to be
larger than for the preceding year. There are indications, however, that
a probable balance might be struck between increases in world cotton seed
oil production and decreases in other edible oils, excluding sunflower seed.
It appears that the 1925 production of sunflower seed, particularly in
Russia, is responsible in a large measure for the indicated potential increased production of all edible oils for 1925. The Russian sunflower seed
area for that year is put at about 6,750,000 acres, according to G. C. Haas,
American Agricultural Commissioner at Vienna, quoting Russian sources. That
figure is said to be 22 per cent greater than 1924, and very much larger
than the pre-war area. Production for 1925 is put at
3,482,000 short tons by the same source, with from 2,500,000 to 2,700,000
short tons said to represent a surplus above domestic needs. This oil is
also readily adaptable to industrial needs, although its use in the United
States for any purpose is negligible.

Supplies of drying oils were definitely larger in 1925 than in 1924,
largely as the result of heavy flaxseed production in Argentina. See
Foreign Crops and Markets, Vol. 12, No. 11. Hempseed is also in larger

THE WORLD VEGETABLE OILS AND OILSEEDS SITUATION, CONT'D.

supply. Heavier United States imports indicate increased supplies of
Chinese wood oil. Decreased crops of soya beans are reported for Manchuria
and Chosen. In general, however, the increase in edible oils capable of
diversion to paints and varnishes may be expected to insure an oil supply
for such purposes.

Trade figures show larger quantities of oils and oilseeds moving
to consuming countries in 1925 than in 1924. For cotton seed alone, an
increase of 16.8 per cent in world imports appears for 1925 over 1924.
World peanut imports increased 35 per cent in the same period. In the
United States oils and oilseeds trade, coconut oil is the leading import
item. Imports of that product for 1925 increased 3.5 per cent over 1924
and 356 per cent over 1913. United States imports of all other vegetable
oils and oilseeds, with the exception of rape and peanut oils, were greater
than in 1924, and also, in most cases, greater than in 1913. Cottonseed
oil is the principal United States vegetable oil export. Figures for that
item in 1925 showed an increase of 44 per cent over 1924, although that trade
is still well below the prewar level.

It has been indicated that the world price level for vegetable oils
and oilseeds declined during 1925 and the early months of 1926. That decline
affected practically all oils adaptable to edible purposes except olive,
Ceylon coconut and refined soya bean oils. Among the recognized technical
oils, linseed led the decline on the strength of the heavy crop of linseed
in Argentina. In the United States, raw linseed oil in tanks dropped 20.7
per cent. In Great Britain, linseed oil declined 32.7 per cent over the same
period.

The manufacture of lard compounds, margarines and soaps involves the
giving of considerable attention to the problem of substitution among the
available vegetable and animal ingredients. Among ingredients of fairly
similar physical and chemical properties, relative price levels alone may
govern almost wholly the degree of substitution. Where ingredients require
considerable processing to adapt them to the manufacture of the finished
product, however, the original market price may be the least important consideration. In general, according to investigations conducted by the United
States Tariff Commission ("Certain Vegetable Oils"; U.S. Tariff Commission,
1926) most technical processes are built around one or two central ingredients,
either animal or vegetable or both. Complete substitutions are rare unless
it is desired to change completely the finished product. Certain percentage
substitutions are made when required and when practicable, however, to utilize
less expensive ingredients when their properties are of the character desired.
Of the non-drying and semi-drying oils produced in the United States, cottonseed is first in importance, both as to price and chemical properties. Corn
oil, while desirable chemically, is generally regarded as too expensive to
produce for use in competition with other oils except as a salad oil, where
it is again second to cottonseed oil. Peanut oil enjoys a comparatively
small demand, since better prices are paid for whole peanuts as a food product.
Soya beans in the United States are still confined largely to use as a forage
crop and soil-builder. See page 647.

THE BRITISH STRIKE AND MARKETS FOR FARM PRODUCTS

The general strike which paralyzed industrial activity in Great Britain from May 4 to 12 was particularly severe in its effect on transportation, making it almost impossible to unload or move imported supplies. Thus for all practical purposes British import trade ceased for a period of eight days. The official settlement of the strike does not mean that the machinery of distribution will run immediately as smoothly as it did before. There will be many days of congestion and confusion with losses of perishable commodities and delayed deliveries of all imported products.

What do the strike and its consequences mean to American agriculture? The direct effects of nine days stoppage of imports will not reduce imports of American farm products as much as might be expected. Of the net value of the products of the farms of the United States, from 10 to 15 per cent are exported, the percentage varying with crop conditions at home and market conditions abroad. In gross value our agricultural exports, excluding forest products, amounted to $1,867,000,000 in the year ending June 30, 1924 and to $2,280,000,000 in the year ending June 30, 1925. Of these amounts exports to the United Kingdom were valued at about $575,000,000 and $675,000,000 respectively, or 31 per cent in each year. Fortunately this is not the season of the heaviest exports of American farm products to the United Kingdom. In May last year American agricultural exports to the United Kingdom amounted to only a little more than $30,000,000 or about 5 per cent of the total for the year ending June 30. Even if there were no exports to the United Kingdom for a month at this season of the year the loss in actual value of export trade would not be a large matter in itself when the whole year's trade is considered, especially when there may be some increase in shipments of some commodities in the next few weeks to replace depleted stocks.

But this is not the whole story. The greatest loss may come from the loss of purchasing power of the British people as a result of the strike and the adjustments that will follow the strike. The cost of the strike cannot be estimated, but it must amount to many millions of dollars each day. This price must eventually be paid either in decreased incomes of capital or labor or both. Some of the loss may possibly be made up by increased production later on, but it is probable that for several months the purchasing power of the British people will be lower than before the strike.

Assuming a decreased purchasing power, how will various imported farm products be affected by the changed situation? The answer is not easy to give. For some products, the market may be even better during a period of low purchasing power than during a period of prosperity. For others, the market will be adversely affected by a decline in purchasing power. Therefore it will be necessary to take up each of the more important commodities separately and examine its relation to the British market situation.

Cotton

Cotton exports to the United Kingdom from the United States in the year ending June 30, 1925 amounted to 2,623,000 bales of 500 pounds valued at $334,751,000. Cotton thus constitutes in value about half of all our

THE BRITISH STRIKE AND MARKETS FOR FARM PRODUCTS, CONT'D.

agricultural exports to the United Kingdom. British imports of raw cotton,
even following the large world crops of the past two years, have been far
below pre-war volume. This reduction in imports has been a consequence of
the decline in British exports of cotton goods. Obviously the closing down
of the mills and the inability of manufacturers to guarantee delivery will
tend to make this situation still worse, and it is also possible that there
will be some decrease in retail sales of cotton goods in the domestic market
as a result of the strike. The effect of the strike, therefore, will be to
decrease exports of American cotton to the United Kingdom. There may be
some corresponding increase in exports to competing countries, but for the
remainder of the present season at least, our cotton exports will probably
fall below the volume which would have been reached under normal conditions.

Wheat and flour

As far as the United States is concerned the market for wheat and
flour is not greatly affected by the strike. American exports of wheat
and flour to the United Kingdom in the nine months ending March 31, 1926
were only about 14,000,000 bushels and there is comparatively little more
wheat available for shipment of the quality demanded by British mills. Canadian
shipments to the United Kingdom for the remaining weeks of the season may be
somewhat curtailed, and there is a possibility that Canadian wheat and flour
may tend to move to other markets where it will compete more directly with
the wheat remaining in stock in the United States.

Pork products

British imports of American pork products have been well maintained
since the war. In 1925 there was a rather heavy decline below 1924, but the
total imports from the United States were still well above the average for
the five years just preceding the world war. American bacon is always
quoted below British, Irish or Danish bacon on the British market. With a
lowering of purchasing power it is possible that there may be some shift in
volume of purchases from the more expensive to the cheaper grades of cured
bacon and hams. In the British market this would favor American pork products,
including lard. A similar situation was observed in Germany following the
inflation period when purchasing power was unusually low. American lard and
bacon for a time were the cheapest fats on the market and were imported in
record quantities with comparatively little use of butter, kettle-rendered
lard, Danish pork products and other more expensive meats and fats. Selling
in an impoverished market, however, may not be profitable, since in order
to obtain volume of sales, prices must be low enough to underbid other competing products.

Corn

Great Britain is not a large consumer of corn and its imports of this
grain in 1925 were little more than half those of 1913. There is, however, a
possibility, which is perhaps even greater because of the losses due to the

THE BRITISH STRIKE AND MARKETS FOR FARM PRODUCTS, CONT'D.

strike, to push the sales of the cheaper grades of corn in Great Britain. As has been noted in a recent release by the United States Department of Agriculture, it is possible to ship No. 3 and No. 4 corn safely to foreign markets. In feeding value this corn is almost as high as the better grades and its price should prove attractive to British purchasers.

Tobacco.

The British market for tobacco has also been well maintained since the war. Imports of American tobacco in 1925 were 163,000,000 pounds as compared with a 1909-13 average of 116,000,000 pounds. The consumption of tobacco seems to have been increased by the war, and it does not seem likely that economic conditions in a country with minimum standards of life as high as in England, would have much effect upon the amount of tobacco consumed. A lowering of purchasing power, however, might lead to a larger demand for cheaper grades.

The British public has shown a very constant preference for American tobacco and there seems to be little danger of competition from other surplus producing countries.

Other agricultural products.

Other imported farm products will feel the effects of the strike in different ways. Such products as fresh fruits, which are classed as luxuries will be likely to suffer as compared with necessities such as oil cake, oats and barley, which must be imported to feed livestock. The season for marketing American apples in England, however, is now practically completed and it is probable that Australian apples will suffer more than ours from the immediate effects of the strike.

Conclusion.

Probably the most serious effect of the recent British general strike from the point of view of American farmers will be in a somewhat decreased demand for raw cotton. For the present season, little American wheat would have been shipped to the United Kingdom under any condition. Pork products exports will suffer a temporary check but are not likely to be reduced greatly in the long run. The same may be said of tobacco and feedstuffs.

The ultimate effects of the adjustements which must follow a general strike cannot be forseen, but with any outcome which now seems within the range of probability the British market for American farm products is likely on the whole to be much the same in the future as in the past. Economies are more likely to be effected in luxuries rather than in necessities, and a large proportion of British agricultural imports from America rank as necessities.

THE BRITISH STRIKE AND MARKETS FOR FARM PRODUCTS, CONT'D.

UNITED KINGDOM: Imports of hams, by countries, average 1909-13, and annual 1923-1925

Country from which imported	Average					Per cent of total Av			
	1909-1913	1923	1924	1925		1909-13	1923	1924	1925
	1,000 pounds	1,000 pounds	1,000 pounds	1,000 pounds		Per cent	Per cent	Per cent	Per cent
United States...	94,241	181,475	165,226	146,685		92.3	92.7	90.2	86.3
Canada.........	7,125	12,802	16,344	21,112		7.0	6.6	8.9	12.4
Other countries.	684	1,397	1,664	2,110		.7	.7	.9	1.3
Total......	102,050	195,674	183,234	169,907		100.0	100.0	100.0	100.0

UNITED KINGDOM: Imports of lard, by countries, average 1909-13, and annual 1923-1925

Country from which imported	Average					Per cent of total Av.			
	1909-1913	1923	1924	1925		1909-13	1923	1924	1925
	1,000 pounds	1,000 pounds	1,000 pounds	1,000 pounds		Per cent	Per cent	Per cent	Per cent
United States...	168,618	234,709	222,053	200,446		85.2	86.0	79.7	78.2
Canada.........	23,557	23,397	29,557	a/		11.9	8.6	10.6	
Other countries.	5,655	14,681	27,158	55,761		2.9	5.4	9.7	21.8
Total......	197,830	272,787	278,768	256,207		100.0	100.0	100.0	100.0

a/ Included in "Other countries."

UNITED KINGDOM: Imports of bacon, by countries, average 1909-13, and annual 1923-1925.

Country from which imported	Average					Per cent of total Av.			
	1909-13	1923	1924	1925		1909-13	1923	1924	1925
	1,000 pounds	1,000 pounds	1,000 pounds	1,000 pounds		Per cent	Per cent	Per cent	Per cent
United States...	197,468	316,810	205,388	166,924		38.6	36.3	23.3	19.9
Denmark	232,527	395,423	446,562	418,749		45.4	45.3	50.6	49.9
Canada.........	47,085	93,440	133,397	141,888		9.2	10.7	15.1	16.9
Other countries.	34,767	67,160	96,471	110,940		6.8	7.7	11.0	13.3
Total.....	511,847	872,833	881,818	838,501		100.0	100.0	100.0	100.0

Compiled from Annual Statement of the Trade of the United Kingdom, 1909-13, and 1923-1924, and Accounts Relating to Trade and Navigation of the United Kingdom, December 1925.

THE BRITISH STRIKE AND MARKETS FOR FARM PRODUCTS, CONT'D

UNITED KINGDOM: Imports of cotton (unmanufactured) by countries, average 1909-13, annual 1923-1925.
(Bales of 478 pounds net)

Country from which imported.	Average 1919-13a/	Year ending December 31						
		1923	1924	1925	Average 1909-13/	1923	1924	1925
COTTON, RAW:	1,000 bales	1,000 bales	1,000 bales	1,000 bales	Per cent	Per cent	Per cent	Per cent
United States	3,574	1,400	1,986	2,560	75.2	51.8	60.2	64.7
Egypt	836	729	722	637	17.6	27.0	21.9	16.1
British India......	155	227	209:b/		3.3	8.4	6.3:b/	
Brazil	63	44	35	78	1.3	1.6	1.1	2.0
Peru	55	162	160:b/		1.2	6.0	4.8:b/	
Other countries ...	65	141	189	681	1.4	5.2	5.7	17.2
Total :..........	4,748	2,703	3,301	3,956	100.0	100.0	100.0	100.0
Reexports :......	584	220	297	286				
Net imports	4,164	2,483	3,004	3,670				
LINTERS: c/								
United States ...		3	12:d/			75.0	85.7:d/	
Germany		1:e/	:d/			25.0:f/	:d/	
Brazil	:e/		1:d/		:f/		7.1:d/	
Other countries	:e/		1:d/		:f/		7.2:d/	
Total		4	14	114		100.0	100.0	100.0
Reexports	:e/	:e/		2				
Net imports ...		4	14	112				

Compiled from "Trade of the United Kingdom" for 1913 and 1924 and "Trade and Navigation of the United Kingdom", December 1925.
a/ Includes "Linters". b/ If any included in "Other countries". c/ Not separately reported for 1909-13. d/ Not available. e/ Less than 500 bales. f/ Less than .05 per cent.

- - - - - -

DECREASE IN ITALIAN HEMP ACREAGE CONFIRMED

Recent cables received in the Department of Agriculture confirm previous reports that the Italian hemp acreage would be below that of last year, and an Italian government statement indicates that the area will be even smaller than has been reported. The International Institute of Agriculture reports an official Italian estimate that the total area will be as small as that of 1924 when about 173,500 acres were cultivated. The indicated reduction of almost 100,000 acres is reported as being sown to sugar beets and potatoes.

Vice-Consul Hurd at Florence, however, cables that private estimates still place the acreage planted in northern Italy at about the same figure as previously estimated, that is, around 155,000 acres, or a reduction of only about 17 per cent from last year. The southern Italian area has previously been reported as only 10 to 15 per cent below last year. These estimates, of course, are unofficial and may not be borne out.

THE BRITISH STRIKE AND MARKETS FOR FARM PRODUCTS, CONT'D
WHEAT, INCLUDING FLOUR: Imports into the United Kingdom,
Calendar years, Average 1909-13, 1923, 1924, 1925

Adjusted to allow for transit shipments and diverted shipments

Country from which imported	Average 1909-13	1923	1924	1925	Per cent of total Av. 1909-13	1923	1924	1925
	1000 bus.	1000 bus.	1000 bus.	1000 bus.	Per cent	Per cent	Per cent	Per cent
United States	29,685	19,511	42,193	17,815	13.4	8.9	17.0	8.6
Canada	62,617	117,691	110,553	107,375	28.3	53.7	44.4	51.9
Argentina	31,462	39,961	45,661	23,426	14.2	18.3	18.3	11.3
Australia	23,235	13,483	24,667	34,433	10.5	6.2	9.9	16.6
Russia	29,076	282	1,406	a/	13.1	.1	.6	-
British India	36,202	23,376	18,323	13,672	16.4	10.7	7.4	6.6
Rumania	1,721	a/	a/	a/	.8			
Other countries	7,470	4,607	6,048	10,213	3.3	2.1	2.4	5.0
Total	221,468	219,011	248,851	206,934	100.0	100.0	100.0	100.0
Domestic production .	59,640	57,423	51,746	52,873				
Total supply	281,108	276,434	300,597	259,807				
Exports	5,790	12,382	19,755	22,387				
Correction for stocks	130:-	2,618:-	8,915:+	11,257				
NET SUPPLY	575,188	261,434	271,927	248,677				

a/ If any, included in "Other countries."
Compiled from Annual Statement of the Trade of the United Kingdom with Foreign Countries, 1909-13, 1923 and 1924, and Accounts Relating to the Trade and Navigation of the United Kingdom, December, 1925. Imports from the United States and Canada adjusted to allow for diverted shipments and in transit shipments.

UNITED KINGDOM: Imports of corn a/ by countries, 1913, and annual
1923-1925

Country from which imported	Year ending December 31				Per cent of total			
	1913	1923	1924	1925	1913	1923	1924	1925
	1,000 bushels	1,000 bushels	1,000 bushels	1,000 bushels	Per cent	Per cent	Per cent	Per cent
Argentina	77,708	39,596	53,670	33,625	79.0	57.4	71.2	60.8
United States .	13,759	10,660	4,091	305	14.0	15.5	5.4	.6
Russia	3,368	38	3,858:b/		3.4	.1	5.1:b/	
Rumania	2,005	2,847	5,593	2,942	2.0	4.1	7.4	5.3
Canada	423	1,611	75	119	.4	2.3	.1	.2
British S.Africa	69	9,528	2,746:b/		.1	13.9	3.6:b/	
Other countries	978	4,699	5,301	18,305	1.1	6.7	7.2	33.1
Total imports	98,310	68,979	73,334	55,296	100.0	100.0	100.0	100.0

Compiled from Annual Statement of the Trade of the United Kingdom with Foreign Countries, 1913, 1923 and 1924, and Accounts Relating to the Trade and Navigation of the United Kingdom, December 1925. a/ Excludes corn flour and meal. b/ If any, included with "Other countries".

INCREASED POTENTIAL SUPPLY OF VEGETABLE OILS

Both edible and inedible vegetable oils were indicated to be in greater potential supply in 1925 than in 1924, according to information on world production of oil-bearing products received to date in the Department of Agriculture. In the case of edible oils, particularly, this situation does not necessarily indicate an increase in the production of oil as an edible product. A clear indication of what the supply of edible oil may be is prevented by the demand existing for such oils for industrial and technical purposes. There is also an important demand for oil bearing products for purposes other than oil production. Also, data are incomplete in some instances on the amount of such oil bearing products now available. For the drying oils, the supply situation can be determined more definitely.

The list of materials yielding edible oils includes cotton seed, peanuts, corn, soya beans, olives, coconuts, sunflower seed and sesamum seed. Other seeds might also be included, but their production bulks so small as to have little or no influence on the potential oil supply. Rapeseed and palm kernels are probably the most important of the minor edible oil producers, but have been omitted from the statistical summary owing to a lack of data. Of the main group, cotton seed and sunflower seed are the two important factors in the indicated increased supply of edible oils. World production of cotton seed for 1925-26 is estimated to be 12 per cent greater than for 1924-25. The estimate of cotton seed production in the United States for 1925-26 is 18/20 per cent greater than for the preceding year. The production of sunflower seed in Russia, the leading producing country, is estimated by Russian authorities to have increased 100 per cent in 1925 over 1924. There is, however, a heavy domestic agricultural and industrial consumption of sunflower seed and its products in Russia. It is a question, therefore, to what extent the increase in that product will affect the international situation in edible oil.

Indications are that the world production of coconuts and soya beans for 1925 may be about equal to or slightly smaller than in 1924, while olive oil production is definitely under that of 1924. A large crop of peanuts in India, the leading producer, probably offsets decreases in that crop reported by other countries. A heavy crop of corn for 1925 in the United States and abroad does not necessarily indicate an increase in the production of corn oil. It is a fact, however, that increased world corn crops in that year, together with a heavy world production of other fodder crops, has increased the potential supply of corn oil.

Flaxseed, the most important of the drying oil seeds under consideration produced a world crop for 1925 exclusive of India, about a fourth greater than in 1924. Argentina is the largest single factor in the increase, with Russia a secondary factor. In India the crop harvested in the spring of 1926 is included with the 1925-26 Argentine crop as part of the 1925 world crop. The India estimate is not yet available but acreage is reported to be 3 per cent below last year. See Foreign Crops and Markets, Vol. 12, No. 11. Hemp seed production is also increased in Russia and Poland, the two most important producing countries, as well as in several minor countries. Cottonseed, soya beans and sunflower seed are also used for paints to a small degree as well as for edible purposes, and the increase in the cotton seed and sunflower seed crops mentioned above adds further to the potential supply of paint and varnish oils.

INCREASED POTENTIAL SUPPLY OF VEGETABLE OIL, CONT'D.

No information is available on production of Chinese wood oil. The United
States, however, is the chief consumer of that product. In the period 1921
to 1924 the United States took about three-fourths of the total exports from
China, imports in 1925 being a fourth larger than in 1924.

Cottonseed:

The 1925 world production of cottonseed amounts to 13,288,000 short tons
according to a preliminary estimate, or 12.1 per cent above the 1924 total of
11,854,000 short tons. This increase is accounted for by the large increase in
the crop of the United States, by far the most important producer, and that of
Russia, which reports an increase of approximately 88.3 per cent over last year
The estimate furnished for the United States is a preliminary one based on the
actual 1924-25 seed production and the increase in the cotton crop of 1925-26
over 1924-25. Reports for India and China, which take second and third place
in this crop, place production slightly below that of 1924, while an increase
is expected in Egypt. World production for the last two years has been above
the average amount produced during the years 1909-13.

Because of the enormous amounts produced, cottonseed is one of the
important sources of margarine and edible oil producing fats, in spite of its
low oil content of 17 - 18 per cent. It is refined in large quantities in
America and Europe for margarine, salad oil and various cooking oils as well
as being hardened and used as an important lard substitute in compounds of the
vegetable-lard type. It is also used in soaps, candles and for various technic
al purposes.

Some idea of the rapid increase in importance of cottonseed products
in the United States may be gained by comparisons of the percentage of seed
crushed compared with total seed production. This percentage has increased
from an average of 12.6 per cent for the years 1881-1885 to 74.7 per cent for
1921-1925. In Egypt most of the cottonseed is exported as seed but the consumption of local crushing factories is becoming of increasing importance.
From 1890-91 to 1894-95 exports of cottonseed averaged 88.2 per cent of the
entire crop while local crushing factories consumed only 2.9 per cent of the
total production. These have now changed to 52.0 and 25.7 per cent respectivel
for the period 1921-22 to 1924-25.

The quantity of oil obtained per ton of seed crushed varies considerably in the different districts. In the western portion of the United States
cotton belt the yield of oil is much lower than in the eastern section. The
average for the United States for the years 1923-1925 was approximately 15 per
cent, according to Bulletin No. 158, Bureau of the Census. The quantity obtained depends upon the variety and condition of the seed and the climatic
conditions during the growing and harvesting seasons, as well as upon the
quantity of oil desired in the cake obtained. The actual supply of cottonseed
oil thus varies from the potential supply which would be available were all
seed crushed under the most favorable conditions. See Table on page 653.

INCREASED POTENTIAL SUPPLY OF VEGETABLE OILS, CONT'D

Rapeseed:

India is the largest producer of rapeseed among the countries for which statistics are available and her average exports from 1910 to 1921 were four times as large as those of China, an important producer for which production figures are lacking. Figures of production for the 1925-26 season in India have not yet been received, but the second acreage estimate is 10.7 per cent below the corresponding estimate of last year. A decided increase is shown in the crop of Rumania, but this total crop is not large enough to influence greatly the world's total supply.

Rape oil has been used extensively as an edible oil in India and during the war the refined oil was used by many European countries in margarine and fat compounds. It is important as a lubricant and illuminating oil. See table on page 652.

Sesamum:

The 1925 sesamum crop of India, the largest producer for which data are available, amounts to 407,000 short tons, which is 27.5 per cent below that of 1924. With the exception of the 1918 crop, the 1925 crop is the smallest reported in the period 1909 - 1925. Precise information as to world supply is not obtainable since no figures are available for China, probably the leading producer, whose average exports from 1910 to 1921 were over 50 per cent higher than those of India.

Sesamum seed produces an oil which is used extensively as a food in India and other countries in which it is produced. It is useful in margarine manufacture and is said to exhibit a very characteristic and simple chemical color test which prevents fraudulent sale of margarine as butter. It is also used as a substitute for olive oil in salad oils. See table on page 657.

Flaxseed:

The 1925 production of flaxseed in 18 countries for which statistical returns have been received to date is estimated at 3,891,916 short tons compared with 3,089,016 short tons produced by the same countries in 1924, an increase of 26 per cent. In 1923 and 1924 these 18 countries produced approximately 83 per cent of the world flax crop and in the five years preceding the war accounted for approximately 80 per cent of world production. The only important country not included in this total is British India, for which no figures are available as yet for the 1925-26 crop. The second estimate of acreage, however, is 3 per cent below the corresponding estimate of last season. The big factor in the 1925 production increase is the large crop in Argentina which amounts to 2,100,000 short tons or 66 per cent above 1924-25 production. During the three years 1922-1924 Argentina produced over 40 per cent of the total world crop. See Foreign Crops and Markets March 15, 1926 for more complete details of the flaxseed situation, and also table on page 661 of this issue.

INCREASED POTENTIAL SUPPLY OF VEGETABLE OIL MATERIALS, CONT'D.

Peanuts:

The 1925-26 peanut crop in India, where in recent years about half of the known peanut crop of the world has been produced is the largest on record and is expected to offset any decrease in the crops of China and the United States for the 1925 season. Production in India in 1925-26 amounted to, 2,137,000 short tons, an increase of 35.6 per cent over the 1,576,000 short tons produced in 1924-25. No estimate is available as yet for China, which country is believed to rank second in peanut production. A report from Trade Commissioner Smiley stated that the commercial crop of China is expected to be 15 per cent below that of 1924. On the other hand, a report from Shantung estimates total production of that district about 25 per cent above last year. Shantung's seaport, Tsingtao, was the leading Chinese port in the export of peanuts for 1922 and 1923. In the United States, production in 1925 was 7.3 per cent below 1924. These three countries in 1921 and 1922 furnished approximately 70 per cent of the reported peanut production of the world. Complete data are not available for Senegal, another important peanut producing country. Exports for 1922 and 1923 were slightly higher than those of 1921 and a large percentage of the estimated crop is exported. The British West Africa Colonies are another source of peanut supply for which figures are not available. The 1925 crop of Nigeria, however, is reported to be approximately equal to that of 1924 when 134,000 short tons were produced.

In considering the peanut as a source of oil it must be remembered that a large portion of the crop, especially in the United States, is not crushed for oil but used in various ways as an article of food in both unmanufactured and manufactured state. Large quantities are produced in Africa for which production estimates are not available. These nuts are mostly consumed locally, however, and so have little effect on the international peanut situation. Peanut oil of fine quality is chiefly used in the manufacture of margarine and other edible fats, being especially important because of its fine keeping qualities. Lower grades of oil, such as those obtained from decorticated kernels of poor quality, are hardened and used in soap manufacture. With peanut oil, as with practically all other oils, a varying amount is used for miscellaneous industrial purposes. See table on page 654.

Coconuts:

The supply of coconuts in 1925, judging by reported production for the Philippine Islands and exports of coconut products from British Malaya and Ceylon in terms of nuts, was slightly larger than that of 1924. The increase for the three countries amounted to approximately 2.3 per cent. These countries accounted for more than 90 per cent of the reported supply of coconuts for the years 1920 to 1924. Although the reported supply is less than the world production, it should be a fair indication of the potential amount available for American and European use in the oils and fats industries.

A considerable decrease in production in 1925 compared with 1924 is reported by the Philippine Islands and a smaller decrease is reported in the exports of British Malaya but these are more than balanced by the increase in exports from Ceylon. Coconut production in the Philippines during the last five

INCREASED POTENTIAL SUPPLY OF VEGETABLE OIL MATERIALS, CONT'D

years has averaged approximately 63.2 per cent above the 1910-1913 average, while exports from Ceylon have increased 81.2 per cent in this period. Early figures for British Malaya are not available for comparison.

In Brazil the coconut industry is developing steadily, according to available figures and consular reports, while an upward trend is also apparent in figures obtained from Trinidad and Tobago.

Coconut oil has, for some time, been an important factor in margarine manufacture and is used for the preparation of salad oils, lard compounds and other edible fat products. Poorer grades are used in soap and candle making. See table on page 655.

Olive Oil:

Production of olive oil for 1925, exclusive of the United States, is estimated at 1,398 million pounds which is 24 per cent below the good harvest of 1,342 million pounds in 1924 and 10 per cent below the 1923 harvest when 1,561 million pounds were produced. See table on page 656.

Soya Beans:

Production of soya beans in 1925 in Manchuria and Chosen was estimated to be 161,000 short tons below the 1924 production in those countries. Manchuria is the world's most important soya bean producer. In 1923 60 per cent of the total reported production was found in Manchuria. Chosen, the only other country for which a report has been received for 1925, shows an increase but it is small compared with the decrease in Manchuria. In 1923 Chosen furnished 20 per cent of the total reported soya bean production. Production in Japan decreased steadily from 1920 to 1923, while the United States has shown important gains during the five years 1920 to 1924. United States figures for 1925 are not yet available. The oil is used in the manufacture of margarine and salad oils and for other edible purposes as well as being used in the soap industry, for paints and various minor technical uses. See table on page 656.

Sunflower Seed:

Commercial production of sunflower seed is determined chiefly by the crop of Russia, the only producer of importance. The crop for 1925 is reported by Russian Authorities to be 3,482,200 short tons, 116.2 per cent above 1924 production. The oil obtained from sunflower seed is useful both as an edible oil and for paints and varnishes. Inferior grades are also used for soap making and other industrial purposes. The seed is used directly as a live stock feed and in some countries, particularly Russia, large quantiti r are used for human consumption. See table on page 657.

INCREASED POTENTIAL SUPPLY OF VEGETABLE OIL MATERIALS, CONT'D

Hempseed:

The production of hempseed in 1925 was much greater than that of 1924 since Russia, the most important producer, reports an increase of 254,000 short tons or 69.7 per cent above 1924. For the period 1909-13 hempseed production in Russia amounted to more than 85 per cent of the reported world total and this proportion had only slightly diminished for the period 1920 to 1924. The increase of the total number of countries so far reporting in 1925 compared with the same countries in 1924 amounts to 66.3 per cent. Hempseed oil is a drying oil used largely as a paint oil and to some extent in soft soaps. According to Louis E. Andes in "Vegetable Fats and Oils" it may be used as an edible oil when fresh. See table on page 661.

- - - - - - -

PRODUCTION OF VEGETABLE OIL MATERIALS AVERAGE 1909-1913, ANNUAL 1920-1925.

Rapeseed *

Estimates of oil content range from 33 to 43 per cent

Country	Average 1909-13 a/	1920	1921	1922	1923	1924	1925
	Short tons	Short tons	Short tons	Short tons	Short tons	Short tons	Short tons
India b/	1,383,000	962,000	1,308,000	1,354,000	1,290,000	1,313,000	c/
Austria	5,936	861	1,160	1,223	1,158	1,293	
Belgium	1,521	2,623	2,159	758	674	612	
Bulgaria	8,154	1,534	673	479	783	115	
Czechoslovakia	10,364	7,940	5,715	4,687	5,274	4,648	4,324
Formosa	345	335	305	68	90		
France d/	51,125	50,074	41,528	30,282	32,828	28,537	
Hungary	12,690	3,032	12,677	8,329	15,882	7,939	
Japan	130,016	115,332	103,098	87,210	78,203		
Netherlands	3,761	7,600	3,166	977	4,755	5,240	4,960
Poland	31,116	26,270	22,520	40,752	52,602	42,924	
Rumania	60,663	26,091	12,328	21,116	18,350	8,640	39,683
Russia(European) e/	34,176						
Yugoslavia	7,000	4,348	4,661	2,126	2,016	1,626	
Total countries reporting 1909-13 to 1924	1,514,667	1,066,282	1,402,259	1,443,613	1,405,972	1,405,934	

*No estimates are available for China one of the leading producing countries.
a/ Where changes in territory have occurred as a result of the world war estimates have been adjusted to correspond with the area within the post-war boundaries.
b/ Includes mustard seed but consists chiefly of rapeseed.
c/ The second estimate of acreage is 10.7 per cent below the corresponding figure for last year. d/ Colza and Navette. e/ Two-year average.

PRODUCTION OF VEGETABLE OIL MATERIALS AVERAGE 1909-1913 ANNUAL 1920-1925, CONT'D.

Cottonseed a/

Estimates of oil content range from 17 to 36 per cent

Country	Average 1909-10 to 1913-14	1920-21	1921-22	1922-23	1923-24	1924-25	1925-26 Prelimin-ary
	Short tons	Short tons	Short tons	Short tons	Short tons	Short tons	Short tons
United States:	5,809,000:	5,971,000:	3,531,000:	4,336,000:	4,502,000:	6,051,000:	b/7,140,000
India........:	1,713,630:	1,440,200:	1,703,900:	2,030,100:	2,065,000:	2,436,400:	2,415,500
China c/.....:d/	332,019:	902,500:	725,100:	1,108,000:	952,600:	1,041,600:	1,010,500
Egypt........:	672,500:	617,800:	446,500:	688,400:	669,300:	739,900:	e/778,700
Russia	:	:	:	:	:	:	
Asiatic.....:	455,534:	27,700:	20,600:	26,300:	30,300:	f/216,500:	f/407,700
Brazil.......:	179,671:	227,600:	241,000:	264,300:	275,300:	289,200:	
Mexico.......:	92,254:	g/h/89,900:	70,400:	85,100:	83,600:	142,400:	102,800
Persia.......:	65,008:	50,200:i/	45,400:i/	45,400:i/	45,400:i/	45,400:	
Turkey, Asiatic...:	63,574:	:	g/14,300:	:	:	:	
Peru.........:	52,530:	83,600:	87,000:	96,000:	97,000:	98,500:	93,000
Uganda......:	9,722:	32,600:	15,000:	37,100:	45,000:	70,000:	
Chosen(Korea):j/	8,311:	48,100:	44,200:	49,400:	53,000:	58,000:	65,500
Argentina....:j/	1,456:	12,600:	13,200:	12,900:	33,000:	32,200:	
Total countries rept.1909-24k/	9,863,000:	9,972,000:	7,320,000:	9,130,000:	9,298,000:	11,728,000:	
Est. world total........:	9,971,000:	10,030,000:	7,380,000:	9,225,000:	9,369,000:	11,854,000:	13,288,000

a/ Computed from estimated lint production counting 2 pounds of seed to 1 pound of lint, except Egypt and the United States which are actual estimates of cottonseed produced. b/ Figure computed by addition of 18 per cent to 1924-25 production to correspond with increase in cotton production. c/ Chinese Economic Bulletin quoting from Chinese Cotton Millowners' Association. d/ Based on commercial crop of cotton as estimated by the United States Bureau of the Census. e/ Based on official estimate of lint. f/ Turkestan, Transcaucasia, Khiva, Bokhara. g/ From an unofficial source. h/ Laguna and Lower California only. i/ Estimated annual production from consular reports. j/ Average for three years. k/ Includes some minor producing countries not listed above.

PRODUCTION OF VEGETABLE OIL MATERIALS AVERAGE 1909-1913, ANNUAL 1920-1925, CONT'D

Peanuts

Estimates of oil content of kernel range from 35 to 50 per cent *, of the unshelled nut 28 per cent.

Peanuts in the Shell

Country	Average 1909-13	1920	1921	1922	1923	1924	1925
	Short tons	Short tons	Short tons	Short tons	Short tons	Short tons	Short tons
India..........	669,100	1,145,000	1,074,000	1,384,000	1,287,000	1,576,000	2,137,00(
China a/.......			325,000	445,000	672,000	672,000: to : 728,000	b/
Argentina......		63,386	46,178	44,969	41,597	53,287	c/
Chosen.........		584	563	548	479	520	
Dutch East Indies d/...		310,226	303,733	288,022	236,597	243,929	
Egypt..........			9,108	8,102	11,119	8,700	10,587
Formosa........	12,634	16,491	19,489				
Japan..........	18,518	22,659	19,130	18,220			
Kwantung.......e/	172	382	476				
Mexico.........				1,443			1,720
Paraguay.......				11,379	10,725	11,376	
Rhodesia.......		1,062	1,063				
Senegal........		315,300	382,300			482,000	
Nigeria........						134,000	f/
Spain.......g/	29,438	32,904	33,069	33,844	33,778	35,342	35,570
Union of South Africa........		7,120	3,750	5,156	7,189		
United States..h/	213,574	420,737	414,654	316,557	323,881	374,462	347,038
Total countries reporting 1921-1924...........			2,206,305	2,521,042	2,606,451	2,964,240: to : 3,020,240	

* Oil content is for the shelled nut. Figures in the table are given in terms of unshelled nuts. The ratio of unshelled to shelled is approximately 1.5 to 1.
a/ Rough estimates supplied by consular service.
b/ The commercial crop was reported by the consular service to be somewhat below 1924.
c/ A good yield is reported according to the International Institute.
d/ Native crop. e/ Three-year average 1911-1913. f/ Crop reported to be approximately equal to 1924. g/ One year only, 1913. h/ One year only 1909.

PRODUCTION OF VEGETABLE OIL MATERIALS AVERAGE 1909-1913, ANNUAL 1920-1925, CONT'D.

COCONUTS*

Estimates of oil content of fresh kernel range from 30 to 40 per cent, copra 60 to 75 per cent.

	Average 1909-13	1920	1921	1922	1923	1924	1925
	Short tons	Short tons	Short tons	Short tons	Short tons	Short tons	Short tons
British Malaya, exports a/ ...:			1,167,900	1,374,400	1,243,600	1,284,400	1,264,400
Ceylon, exports b/ ...:	809,700	1,091,300	1,132,100	1,337,200	1,052,600	1,396,000	1,609,500
Philippines :c	1,046,588	1,696,072	1,738,857	1,649,083	1,702,531	1,771,493	1,680,330
Australia ..:		212:	160:	423.	377:		
Brazil......:		43,028:	81,350:	95,412:	97,405:		
British Guiana...			17,628:	25,115:	17,891:	13,824:	
British Honduras...:		Average production 9,000 short tons					
Dutch East Indies.....:		9,431:	6,223:	7,294:	8,728:	10,425:	
Dutch Guiana:d/	924:	2,909:	2,490:	2,365:	2,334:	2,433:	
Guatemala...:				477:			
Jamaica.....:		31,740:	27,218:	34,158:	26,636:	24,233:	
Kenya Colony:		252:	391:	535:	626:	749:	
Panama......:		11,910:	12,584:	14,270:	14,157:	11,236:	
Seychelles..:d/	29,213:	28,090:	29,621:	661:		4,497:	
Trinidad and: Tobago.....:d/	22,472:	48,315:	37,079:	52,809:	60,674:		
Total Philippines pro. & Br. Malaya & Ceylon exports			4,038,857:	4,360,683:	3,998,731:	4,451,893:	4,554,280
Total all coun. reptg. incl. Ceylon exports & British Malaya exports 1921-1923...:			4,223,980:	4,593,064:	4,227,559:		

*Estimated weight in short tons converted, except for Brazil, from the number of coconuts on the basis of 890 nuts to the short tons according to the estimate of the International Institute of Agriculture in Oleaginous Products and Vegetable Oils 1921, p. XXV, 1 long ton = 1,000 nuts.
a/ Figures for British Malaya are rough estimates of exports of copra and coconut oil reduced to a basis of nuts used. Shipments of whole nuts are not included but amounted to 14,600 short tons in 1924 and 14,700 short tons in 1925. b/ Figures for Ceylon are rough estimates of exports obtained by reducing oil desiccated coconut and copra to a basis of nuts used. Shipments of whole nuts are not included but have ranged from 10,763 in 1920 to 32,250 in 1924, hence are small in comparison with exports of coconut products. Production of nuts in Ceylon amounted to 1,899,159 short tons for 1911-13 average and 1,077,155 short tons in 1921. c/ Four-year average 1910-1913. d/ 1913.

PRODUCTION OF VEGETABLE OIL MATERIALS AVERAGE 1909-1913, ANNUAL 1920-1925, CONT'D

Olive Oil

Country	Average 1909-13	1920	1921	1922	1923	1924	1925 Preliminary
	1,000 pounds	1,000 pounds	1,000 pounds	1,000 pounds	1,000 pounds	1,000 pounds	1,000 pounds
Spain...........:	484,345	698,778:	608,580:	637,381:	659,885:	708,959:	689,230
Italy..........:	390,000	403,980:	319,980:	557,930:	391,900:	459,660:	330,700
Greece.........:		315,409:	98,457:	216,081:	107,630:	307,700:	126,560
France.........:		11,530:	20,830:	19,810:	31,770:	18,000:	15,430
Portugal.......:a/	50,138	39,200:	51,020:	63,930:	95,990:	69,730:	54,040
Palestine......:		14,770:	1,320:	7,280:	8,570:	10,810:	7,500
Syria..........:		52,250:	53,570:	33,190:	26,430:	22,930:	9,740
Turkey.........:				100,508:	98,900:	77,000:b/	(18,000)
Algeria........:	66,972	67,914:	51,169:	56,133:	69,189:	51,490:	55,140
Tunis..........:c/	67,104	99,210:	74,960:	40,100:	48,500:	48,500:	65,930
Morocco........:		11,530:	12,920:	13,490:	15,870:	19,180:	15,430
Cyprus.........:		25,930:	923:	1,170:	2,310:	6,160:b/	(4,300)
Yugoslavia.....:		908:	1,073:	12,734:	7,010:	11,320:b/	(8,000)
United States d/ e/	965	651:	1,049:	585:	574:	1,528:	
Total countries reporting 1920-1925.........:		1,742,060:	1,295,851:	1,658,813:	1,462,558:	1,765,967:	1,380,000

a/ 1911. b/ Figures in parenthesis are rough estimates based on reports of relation of crop to that of 1924. c/ 1911-13 average. d/ Factory production as reported by the Bureau of the Census. e/ 1912 only.

Soya Beans

Estimates of oil content range from 10 to 21 per cent

Country	Average 1909-13	1920	1921	1922	1923	1924	1925
	Short tons	Short tons	Short tons	Short tons	Short tons	Short tons	Short tons
China – Manchuria....:		3,862,000:	1,950,000:	3,272,000:	2,500,000:	2,534,000:	2,275,000
Chosen a/......:	499,119:	735,784:	718,598:	693,497:	712,790:	561,701:	650,000
Dutch East Indies b/.....:		112,193:	110,899:	113,622:	107,223:	108,108:	
Japan..........:	533,239:	655,785:	654,424:	558,711:	527,342:	d/	
Kwantung.......:d/	17,507:	11,564:	18,162:				
United States :		68,340:	84,450:	174,960:	268,320:	287,010:	
Total countries reporting 1920-1924 :		4,778,317:	2,863,947:	4,254,079:	3,588,333:	3,490,819:	

a/ Four-year average 1910-1913. b/ Native crop. c/ Exports for 1924 were 5.2 per cent below 1923 exports, but the amount exported is insignificant compared with the total production. d/ Three-year average 1911-1913.

PRODUCTION OF VEGETABLE OIL MATERIALS AVERAGE 1909-1913, ANNUAL 1920-1925, CONT'D

Sunflower Seed

Estimates of oil content range from 21 to 50 per cent

Country	Average 1909-13 a/	1920	1921	1922	1923	1924	1925
	Short tons	Short tons	Short tons	Short tons	Short tons	Short tons	Short tons
Russia(European) b/	395,960			):1,669,980:d/	1,897,100:d/	1,610,500:d/	3,482,200:d/
Russia(Asiatic) c/	7,094			):			
Austria	53						
Bulgaria		3,466	2,940	7,060		13,210	
Hungary						21,122	
Rumania c/	3,822		12,295	27,623	59,655		
Union of S.Africa		1,782	1,248				
Yugoslavia	19						
Australia	34						
Southern Rhodesia		1,160	351				

a/ Where changes in territory have occured as a result of the world war, estimates
have been adjusted to correspond with the area within post-war boundaries.
b/ Three-year average, 1911-1913.
c/ Two-year average, 1912-1913.
d/ Includes Asiatic Russia.

Sesamum *

Range of estimate of oil content 35 to 55 per cent

Country	Average 1909-13	1920	1921	1922	1923	1924	1925
	Short tons	Short tons	Short tons	Short tons	Short tons	Short tons	Short tons
India	525,800	428,000	580,000	540,000	488,000	561,000	407,000
Bulgaria	a/ 818	935	931	1,330	728	2,201	
Chosen		4,480					
Egypt				5,688	5,208	4,821	
Formosa	3,763	2,894	1,592				
Greece		3,990	2,712				
Japan				4,066			
Mexico				4,969			7,000
Siam		362	984	914	1,008	607	
Tanganyika		1,852	1,003	1,551			

* No estimates are available for China one of the leading producing countries.
a/ Estimate has been adjusted to correspond with the area within post-war boundaries.

PRODUCTION OF VEGETABLE OIL MATERIALS AVERAGE 1909-1913, ANNUAL 1920-1925, CONT'D

Palm Kernel Exports *

Estimates of oil content range from 35 to 50 per cent

Country	Average 1909-13 Short tons	1919 Short tons	19.. Short tons	Short tons	Short tons	Short tons	Short tons
British West Africa –							
Gold Coast....:	14,203:	11,080:	8,584:	1,849:	3,534:	3,870:	5,110
Gambia......:	513:	752:	524:	338:	504:	439:	
Nigeria......:	194,338:	242,943:	231,858:	171,756:	200,170:	260,033:	
Sierra Leone..:	51,245:	56,697:	56,476:	45,258:	54,912:	66,690:	67,840
French W.Africa –							
Dahomey......:	37,703:	76,039:	32,343:	27,803:	37,809:	40,749:	
Fr. Guinea....:	5,175:	13,765:	8,286:	7,435:	10,765:	10,331:	
Ivory Coast ..:a/	6,730:	18,120:	12,088:	6,563:	9,472:	13,230:	
Senegal......:	1,681:	4,369:	1,454:	3,288:	2,753:	3,343:	
French Equatorial							
Gaboon......:	525:	:d/	833:	1,403:	2,481:	1,777:	
Middle Congo :b/	6:	8,384:	5,097:	4,142:	4,271:	6,122:	
Ubangi Chari :	:	:	:	:	598:	1,036:	
French Mandatory:							
Cameroon......:	17,119:	42,550:	24,884:	21,049:	:	:	
French Togo...:	10,423:	15,794:	11,462:	1,786:	6,800:	:	
Portuguese Africa							
Portuguese							
Guinea......:a/	64,453:	:	:	:	:	:	
Angola.......:	2,939:	:	:	:	:	:	
Spanish Guinea :							
& Fernando Po .:c/	210:	274:	:	:	:	:	
Belgian Congo :a/	7,166:	41,131:	43,494:	:	:	:	
Dutch East							
Indies, pro. :	:	:	373:	168:	565:	802:	1,247
Total countries							
reporting 1909- :							
13 to 1923......:	311,594:	432,149:	356,710:	268,432:	324,190:	404,807:	

* Figures for the Dutch East Indies are actual production figures. For other countries export figures have been used since production figures are not available.
a/ Four-year average 1910-1913. b/ Two-year average 1910-1911.
c/ Three-year average 1911-1913. d/ Second half only of 1920.

PRODUCTION OF VEGETABLE OIL MATERIALS AVERAGE 1909-1913, ANNUAL 1920-1925, CONT'D

Palm oil exports *

Country	:Average :1909-13	1919	1920	1921	1922	1923	1924
	Short tons	Short tons	Short tons	Short tons	Short tons	Short tons	Short tons
British W. Africa -							
Gold Coast	7,093	4,204	2,820	223	942	1,584	1,837
Nigeria	89,253	113,083	95,039	59,104	98,122	111,372	
Sierre Leone ...	3,197	3,713	2,314	214	2,325	3,748	3,428
French W. Afria -							
Dahomey	14,282	24,815	12,579	5,389	12,836	15,103	
Fr. Guiena	92	839	451	566	613	883	
Ivory Coast	6,738	14,084	9,540	4,278	7,485	8,829	
Senegal	-	-	12	15	8	3	
French Equatorial							
Gaboon	97				77	214	
Middle Congo ...	23	239	255	276	257	255	
French Mandatory -							
Cameroon	3,977	4,226	2,921	1,835			
French Togo	3,175	2,840	3,298	123	1,048		
Portuguese Africa -							
Portuguese Guinea:a/	26						
Angola .... :b/	290						
Spanish Guinea and							
Fernando Po .... :c/	44	1					
Belgian Congo ...	2,314	8,818	8,404				
Dutch East Indies,							
pro.	d/	e/	1,659	2,368	4,212	4,270	5,428
Total countries re-							
porting 1909-13 to							
1924,incl. Dutch							
East Indies	120,678	160,977	124,657	72,418	126,792	146,044	

* Figures for the Duch East Indies are actual production figures. For other
countries export figures have been used, since production figures are not available.
a/ Four-year average, 1910-1913.
b/ Two-years only, 1909 and 1912.
c/ Three-year average 1911-1913.
d/ Not produced on a commercial scale.
e/ First year in which the crop was produced on a commercial scale.

PRODUCTION OF VEGETABLE OIL MATERIALS AVERAGE 1909-1913, ANNUAL 1920-1925, CONT'D

Poppy Seed *

Estimates of oil content range from 41 to 50 per cent

Country	:Average :1909-13 : a/	1920	1921	1922	1923	1924	1925
	: Short : tons	Short tons	Short tons	Short tons	Short tons	Short tons	Short tons
Austria .... :	1,123 :	1,027 :	1,016 :	1,263 :	1,193 :	1,433 :	
Bulgaria .... :	90 :	315 :	179 :	138 :	(125):	105 :	
Czechoslovakia ..... :	6,496 :	10,482 :	6,277 :	6,085 :	8,681 :	7,338 :	
France .... :	4,607 :	925 :	916 :	710 :	713 :	398 :	
Hungary .... :	:	:	:	:	4,139 :	2,918 :	
Netherlands .... :	:	1,898 :	1,362 :	4,195 :	3,785 :	3,102 :	
Rumania .... :	29 :	:	286 :	46 :	98 :	:	
Yugoslavia ....:	790 :	1,326 :	1,236 :	1,717 :	1,480 :	1,418 :	
Poland .... :	356 :	:	1,020 :	:	1,882 :	:	
Total countries reporting 1909-13 to 1924 .... :	13,106 :	14,075 :	9,624 :	9,913 :	12,192 :	10,692 :	

* No estimates are available for India and Russia, large producing countries, and
such minor countries as Macedonia, Turkey, Persia and China.
a/ Where changes in territory have occured as a result of the world war estimates
have been adjusted to correspond with the area within the post-war boundaries.

Mustard Seed

Estimates of oilcontent range from 21 to 33 per cent

Country	:Average :1909-13	1920	1921	1922	1923	1924	1925
	: Short : tons	Short tons	Short tons	Short tons	Short tons	Short tons	Short tons
Czechoslovakia .... :	:	4,172 :	671 :	655 :	757 :	705 :	
Netherlands .... :	3,396 :	4,034 :	1,176 :	2,727 :	2,505 :	3,817 :	
Rumania .... :	16 :	:	238 :	1 :	:	:	

In most countries mustard seed is included in statistics of rape seed production. I
is therefore impossible to give a separate total for mustardseed. India is known to
be by far the largest producer.

PRODUCTION OF VEGETABLE OIL MATERIALS. AVERAGE 1909-1913, ANNUAL 1920-1925, CONT'D

Flaxseed

Estimates of oil content range from 30 to 40 per cent

Country	Average 1909-13 a/	1922	1923	1924	1925
	Short tons	Short tons	Short tons	Short tons	Short tons
Argentina ....:	871,276	1,332,156	1,624,140	1,262,352	2,100,000
India ....:	576,184	595,960	517,440	605,920	b/
United States ....:	547,204	290,500	477,680	887,903	616,196
Canada...............:	337,120	140,252	199,920	271,460	260,316
Russia ....:	531,552	309,232	374,892	462,644	683,940
Total, 5 countries .....:	2,863,336	2,689,100	3,194,072	3,490,284	
Estimated world total ..:	3,122,000	2,878,400	3,430,000	3,763,200	

a/ Where changes in territory have occured as a result of the world war estimates
have been adjusted to correspond with the area within the post-war boundaries.
b/ Second estimate of acreage is 3 per cent below the corresponding estimate for 1924.

Hempseed

Estimates of oil content range from 16 to 35 per cent of seed

Country	Average 1909-13 a/	1920	1921	1922	1923	1924	1925
	Short tons	Short tons	Short tons	Short tons	Short tons	Short tons	Short tons
Russia .... :	421,349	282,630	240,445	323,492	371,255	364,641	618,665
Austria .... :	523	55	30	122	113	212	
Belgium ....:	52			149	69	45	52
Bulgaria ...... :	1,291	1,823	1,524	1,041	1,984	1,960	1,435
Chile .... :		1,596	1,768	1,484	1,250	1,229	
Czechoslovakia :	4,129	4,757	5,034	5,679	6,921	5,829	7,929
France	7,725	4,092	2,996	2,349	1,474	1,424	2,047
Hungary .... !	6,575	4,950	5,745	4,565	3,540	5,183	
Latvia .... :	524				147		
Lithuania ..... :	1,476	24	9				3,086
Poland.......... :	19,445	13,108	18,551	28,505	32,253	25,550	37,700
Rumania........ :	20,100	9,373	16,984	19,414	15,084	15,595	
Spain .... :		8,713	7,120	15,285	10,002	4,240	3,675
Yugoslavia .... :	8,210						
Netherlands ... :	25	23	8				
Total countries reporting 1909-13 to 1924, incl. Spain and Chile :	481,137	330,102	301,247	401,935	443,876	425,863	

a/ Where changes in territory have occured as a result of the world war estimates
have been adjusted to correspond with the area within the post-war boundaries.

Foreign Crops and Markets Vol. 12, No. 20

PRODUCTION AND DISTRIBUTION OF THE EGYPTIAN COTTONSEED CROP

Cotton season : September to August	Stock remaining from previous season	Crop	Exported	Consumption of local crushing factories	Used for sowing
	Short tons	Short tons	Short tons	Short tons	Short tons
Average, 1910-11 to 1914-15 *	5,482	697,597	512,935	116,734	68,596
Average, 1915-16 to 1919-20 *	8,692	542,085	284,147	129,304	68,195
1920-21	39,446	617,769	304,472	122,350	54,556
1921-22	32,092	446,478	259,543	155,913	76,218
1922-23	37,708	688,371	390,050	165,407	72,608
1923-24	15,377	669,254	329,479	175,036	75,684
1924-25	2,808	739,856	360,902	194,291	81,434

Ministry of Finance, Statistical Department; Monthly Agricultural Statistics, Egypt, October 1924, and October 1925, page 36.
* For details of yearly distribution 1910-11 to 1919-20 see Foreign Crops and Markets April 6, 1925, page 368.

- - - - -

PRODUCTION OF OIL PALM PRODUCTS IN THE DUTCH EAST INDIES AND IN NIGERIA

Production of oil palm products in the Dutch East Indies by plantation methods, although still insignificant in amount, is attracting much attention because of the rapidity with which the industry is expanding. 1919 was the first year in which the products were exported in merchantable quantity. From 1920 to 1924 production of palm oil has increased from 1,659 short tons to 5,428 short tons or 227 per cent. The bearing area increased only about 50 per cent during the period 1919 to 1923, according to Consul Redeker at Medan, but new plantations were being started and the total planted area in 1923 was three times as great as in 1919, which indicates that production may be expected to increase materially for several years at least. The area figures quoted exclude one important plantation for which estimates were not available. It has been roughly estimated that figures for this company would increase the total planted area of 1923 by something like 20 per cent. Additional plantations were either in course of preparation or were being planned for.

This expansion is being watched with special interest by those interested in African oil palm products which have previously had almost a monopoly on the trade. It is particularly interesting in view of the possible analogy between its increase and the rapid increase in plantation rubber production in the East Indies with its serious effect on the Brazilian wild rubber industry.

PRODUCTION OF PALM PRODUCTS IN THE DUTCH EAST INDIES AND IN NIGERIA, CONT'D

The industry in the Dutch East Indies, Consul Redeker states, is unlike that of Africa in that cultivation is carried on throughout on European-managed plantations, using scientific methods of production and manufacture of the product. Most of these plantations are held by the operating companies under concession for 75 years and worked with a system of coolie labor under three-year contracts. Most of the estates also grow other products as well, such as rubber, tobacco, tea, coffee or sisal. In Nigeria, on the other hand, the land is recognized as belonging entirely to the natives and any rights acquired by foreigners must be negotiated with the native owners, subject to the covering approval of the Government, according to the Times Trade and Engineering Supplement of March 21, 1925. Only short term leases are permitted and on their expiration the plant must be forfeited or removed if the native lessor declines to renew the issue. The system has resulted so far in keeping the industry largely in the hands of the natives.

The oil palm in west Africa is a wild tree or at most only semi-cultivated, growing in a dense tropical undergrowth which makes access difficult. It also forces the trees to grow to a great height, making skilled climbers necessary. In the East Indies the trees, spaced at regular intervals, are kept free of undergrowth. The palms, relieved of the necessity of struggling for light and air, do not grow to a great height and the difficulty of climbing and collection is minimized. The yield per tree is also greater in the East Indies.

A much larger portion of the oil is recovered in the Indies than in Nigeria and the free fatty acids are reduced to a minimum. Palm oils having a free fatty acid as low as three to four per cent are said to be usable for edible purposes and part of the East Indies product conforms to this requirement and forms an excellent basis for the preparation of substitute butter and cooking fats. In Nigeria the oil is accumulated in small quantities from day to day in the villages and fresh oil and oil which has become partially rancid are mixed, impairing the quality of the whole. By the primitive methods used a high fatty acid percentage results. The Times Trade Supplement states that many of the native oils contain as much as 40 per cent free fatty acid although if carefully prepared these methods may yield an oil with as low as 10 per cent oil fatty acid. It further states that by African hand methods 35 to 40 per cent of soft oil is extracted and (or) 50 per cent of hard, as compared with at least 90 per cent by machine methods. The quantity of kernels actually exported shows that the export of oil is less than a fourth of what might be recovered from the fruit.

THE PALM KERNEL INDUSTRY IN SIERRA LEONE.

A report from Vice Consul C. E. Macy states that Sierra Leone's annual palm kernel production is estimated at approximately 60,000 tons (kind of ton not stated). It is further estimated, he states, that this production could be obtained from an area 360 square miles in extent if the yield per acre was only half as good as that from the "Eastern" plantations, (Dutch East Indies and British Malaya), that is to say, from an area amounting to not more than 2% of the total area of the protectorate; as it is, the palm nuts are gathered from an area 6 to 10,000 square miles in extent.

The yield could easily be increased by the introduction of the "plantation" system. Such a scheme would present no insurmountable obstacles from a technical or financial standpoint, but a question of policy does intervene. Under the "plantation" system the role of the native becomes limited to that of a laborer, who cares for the trees and collects the fruit. This is in opposition to the government's long declared policy of encouraging the individual native farmer and non-interference so far as possible with already installed native rights and customs.

The policy now contemplated therefore, is, in principle, to encourage the native producers to take proper care of their palms. It is estimated that the present yield is only 1/10 of what it would be were the palm fruits protected from fires started when the annual "burnings-off" for new food-stuff farms occur. However, the natives will never be induced to take up improved methods until it is proved to them by actual demonstration that taking care of their palms pays.

The colonial government's plan is, therefore, to establish palm forest reserves of about 2,000 acres in extent in each of the three provinces of the Protectorate, and to improve the palm stands in such areas by

(a) cutting out the old unproductive trees and replacing them with young palms of a demonstrated oil-yielding species

(b) clearing the undergrowth, and cleaning up the heads of the palms where the fruit clusters

(c) planting vacant areas to young trees, and

(d) eliminating the thick rind varieties which yield little pericarp.

More than 95% of the palm kernels exported are destined for the United States.

OIL CONTENT OF OIL-BEARING SEEDS

In order to determine the importance of the various vegetable oil materials it is necessary to know not only the amount of materials but some measure of the relative amount of oil that can be obtained from the various materials as well. This measure is difficult to obtain due to the variation in oil content and in the amount of oil extracted. The amount of oil contained in the seeds varies with variations in climatic conditions in the different countries and within any country it varies with variations in growing conditions from season to season. The amount of oil actually extracted varies more widely due to differences in the methods of pressing or extraction and in the machinery used, and the uses to which the products are put.

The following estimates collected from various sources are helpful in indicating the general range of content and yield of the various oils. The sources do not always state definitely whether the figures refer to oil content or to actual oil extraction. The figures given by the Bureau of Plant Industry are approximate averages based in most cases on a large number of determinations.

Name of Seed	Louis E. Andes a/ Per cent of oil e/	Frank Fehr b/ Per cent of oil	Paul Blatt-man c/ Per cent of oil	Bolton and Polly d/ Per cent of oil	Per cent of	Estimates collected by the Bureau of Plant Industry, U. S. D. A. Bibliography
Cottonseed :	24-36 :	18 :	18 :	:	17	:U.S.D.A. Bulletin 769, page 12.
Flaxseed . :	38-40 :	30 :	30 :	35 :	35-38	: " " " " 28.
Soybeans . :	:	10 :	10 :	f/ 10 :	14-21	: " " " " 25
Peanuts,	:	:	:	:		:
decorticated	43-45 :	35 :	32 :	:		:
United States	:	:	:	:	::	
Spanish ..:	:	:	:	:	50	:Thompson, H.C. and Daily, H.S.,
Virginia.:	:	:	:	:	41.7	:Farmers Bulletin 751.
Gambia ... :	:	:	:	:	44-45	: " " "
Bombay ... :	:	:	:	:	36-38	: " " "
Mozambique :	:	:	:	:	40-42	: " " "
Sesamum .. :	50-57 :	45 :	35 :	:	50	:Office Report, J.H.Shrader 1918,
:	:	:	:	:		: page 22.
Rapeseed	:	:	:	:		:Levkowitsch, "Oils, Fats and
(Colza) . :	35-43 :	35 :	35 :	:	33-43	:Waxes".
Hempseed . :	30-35 :	30 :	30 :	30 :	16-30	: " " " " "
Mustard,	:	:	:	:		:
black ... :	31-33 :	:	34 :	:	31-33	: " " " " "
Poppy .... :	41-50 :	:	48 :	:	45-50	: " " " " "
Sunflower :	21-22 :	30 :g/	30 :	22-25 :	45-50	:U.S.D.A. Bulletin 769, page 30.
Coconut, .:	:	:	:	:		:
fresh kernel	40-45 :	:	:	:	30-40	:Levkowitsch "Oils, Fats & Waxes
Copra .... :	:	65 :	65 :	:	60-75	:Office Circular, J.H.Shrader,
:	:	:	:	:		:"Notes on Coconut Oil Pressing"
Palm ..... :	:	:	:	:	58-66	:Ber. d.d. pharm. Ges., 1903,p.115

Continued -

OIL CONTENT OF OIL-BEARING SEEDS, CONT'D

Name of Seed	Louis E. Andes a/	Frank Fehr b/	Faure Blatt- man c/	Bolton and Pelly d/	Estimates collected by the Bureau of Plant Industry, U. S. D. A.	
	Per cent of oil	Per cent of oil	Per cent of oil	Per cent of oil	Per cent of oil	Bibliography
Palm nut ..	45-50	45	45		35-40	Cotton Oil Press 4, October 19:
Olive	40-65				35-65	Calif. Sta. Bul. 158, p. 25
Castor Bean	46-53	42	42	50	42-58	U.S.D.A. Bul. 867, p. 2

a/ Vegetable Fats and Oils, Louis E. Andes, London, 1925. b/ Review of the Oilseeds and Oil Markets for 1925, London 1925. c/ Review of the Oil and Fat Markets for 192! Faure, Blattman & Co., London, January 1926. d/ Oil, Fats, Waxes and Resins. E. R. Bolton and R. G. Pelly. "Resources of the Empire Series" London 1924. e/ The oil actually produced compared with seeds crushed in the United States for the years 192: to 1925 as reported by the Bureau of the census shows a yield of approximately 15 per cent. f/ This figure is for oil extracted from beans used. The same source states that the beans generally contain from 16 to 19 per cent of oil. g/ Unclassified see including sunflower.

- - - - - - -

GENERAL PRICE DECLINE IN OILS AND OILSEEDS

The trend of prices of most oilseeds and their products has been downward sin January 1925, at which time the general price level was higher than at any other per since the middle of 1920. The present levels are comparable in many respects to tho prevailing in January 1917. In the period 1917 to 1926, the high point was reached most vegetable oils in June, 1919, with the low point coming in April 1921. From th period the recovery was more or less constant until the coming of the present period of lower prices. The notable exceptions to the downward movement are copra and coco nut oil, rapeseed and rapeseed oil, and olives and olive oil.

In the United States, crude cotton seed oil in southeastern tanks declined 13 per cent from April 1925 to April 1926, according to the New York "Oil, Paint and Dr Reporter". Crude corn oil, in barrels, dropped off 2 per cent during the same perio Coconut oil, an important oleo ingredient, shows a price increase of 2 per cent in barrels. Olive oil, in barrels, rose 5.2 per cent over the period indicated. In th drying and semi-drying oils group, the Minneapolis price of $2.33 per bushel for lin seed in March 1926 showed a decline below March 1925 of 65 cents or 21.8 per cent. The March 1926 figure, however, was 40 cents and 81 cents in excess of Winnipeg and Buenos Aires respectively. See Foreign Crops and Markets, Vol. 12, No. 11. Raw lin seed oil in tanks registered a price decline of 20.7 per cent for the period April 1925 to April 1926, corresponding closely with the linseed movement. Chinese wood oil in barrels at New York, also declined during that period to the extent of 21 per cen Soya beans and oil, however, have not followed the direction of other oil products. The C.I.F. price of Manchurian soyabeans at Pacific Coast ports moved upward dur-

GENERAL PRICE DECLINE IN OILS AND OILSEEDS, CONT'D

ing most of the year ended March 31,1926, but reacted to $1.57 per bushel of 60 pounds, at the end of the year, a net increase over March 1925 of 3.8 per cent. Crude soya bean oil, in barrels, was quoted last month at the same figure as for April 1925.

In Great Britain, a leading foreign market for vegetable oils and oilseeds, conditions similar to those existing in the United States have prevailed for the last twelve months. In that market the same general tendency toward lower price levels is evident. Crude peanut oil, largely of East Indian origin, was quoted last month at prices more than 10 per cent under those of April 1925, according to the London "Grocer and Oil Trade Review." Crude cottonseed oil dropped off 7.8 per cent, with the English refined product declining 6.6 per cent on its price during the year ended April 30, 1926. Refined rapeseed registered a loss of 1.9 per cent for the period mentioned. Coconut oil, however, showed an increase of 2.1 per cent. Among the drying oils, linseed is outstanding with a loss amounting to 32.7 per cent of the price level for April 1925. Crude soya bean oil, however, declined only 2.3 per cent during the last 12 months, while Chinese wood oil prices dropped only 3.6 per cent.

It is obvious that no two vegetable oils have exactly similar properties. There are many cases, however, where the properties of two or more oils admit of their being substituted to a greater or less degree to produce the same finished product. In such cases the question of relative price is of outstanding importance. According to the recent investigations conducted by the United State Tariff Commission ("Certain Vegetable Oils"; 1926), soya-bean oil represents an interesting case of possible substitution in that its properties admit of its use in paints, food and soap. It is the principal link between the paint oil group of vegetable oils and the food and soap groups. Before the passage of the tariff act of May, 1921, the relatively low price of Oriental soya-bean oil admitted of its use to a considerable degree in the three industries mentioned, particularly in soap making. Since 1921 its use in the United States has been reduced to a comparatively negligible quantity.

Price movements of coconut oil are of outstanding importance to the soap industry, which is the largest consumer of that commodity in the United States. This product comes largely from the Philippine Islands, duty free. For the production of high grade white soaps, according to the commission, there appears to be no generally accepted substitute for coconut oil, although some manufacturers suggest palm-kernel oil as the best alternative. Other possible substitutes are tallow, grease, palm oil, cotton oil and olive oil. The margarine industry in the United States also views coconut oil as its leading vegetable ingredient. Cottonseed comes next, with peanut oil, corn oil and soya-bean oil following in the order named, in addition to the essential animal oils and fats. The vegetable oils mentioned are used in proportions varying with their availability at any given time. In the lard compound industry, cottonseed oil is the outstanding raw material, animal or vegetable. Here coconut takes second place, followed by corn, peanut and soya-bean oils, their relative importance always subject to the prices prevailing for each.

GENERAL PRICE DECLINE OF OILS AND OIL SEEDS, CONT'D

COTTONSEED OIL, PRIME SUMMER YELLOW: Average spot price per pound
(barrels), New York; average 1909-13, annual 1921 to 1926

Month	Average 1909-13	\multicolumn{6}{Year beginning September}					
		1921	1922	1923	1924	1925
	Cents	Cents	Cents	Cents	Cents	Cents
September ..	7.50	8.69	9.96	10.34	13.83	11.09
October	7.41	9.88	8.54	11.62	10.54	10.81
November ...	6.78	8.69	8.88	12.01	11.00	9.86
December ...	6.58	8.30	9.51	11.67	10.86	10.32
January	6.62	8.28	9.81	11.00	11.41	10.47
February ...	6.65	8.62	10.77	11.00	11.10	11.33
March	6.64	9.86	10.90	10.03	10.69	11.28
April	6.72	11.48	11.78	9.77	11.10	12.24
May	6.98	11.57	11.76	10.09	11.08	
June	7.18	11.71	11.60	9.82	10.51	
July	7.25	11.33	11.48	10.42	10.75	
August	7.47	10.97	10.35	11.98	11.38	
Average	6.98	9.95	11.44	10.81	11.19	

Division of Statistical and Historical Research. January 1909-December 1921 from
annual reports of the New York Produce Exchange; 1922 and subsequently, compiled from
Oil, Paint and Drug Reporter, average of daily ranges.

COTTONSEED OIL (REFINED, NAKED): Average monthly prices, per pound
at Hull, England, 1913 and 1920 to 1925

Month	1913	1921	1922	1923	1924	1925
	Cents	Cents	Cents	Cents	Cents	Cents
January	5.65	6.20	7.40	8.55	8.79	10.78
February	5.98	6.48	7.86	8.88	9.38	9.96
March	5.93	6.31	8.52	8.92	8.86	9.33
April	6.11	5.70	8.77	9.30	8.55	9.37
May	6.24	6.53	9.58	9.19	8.27	9.69
June	6.41	6.74	9.09	8.45	8.15	9.76
July	7.33	7.42	9.06	8.29	8.58	10.03
August	7.55	7.56	8.45	8.25	9.29	10.27
September	7.05	8.19	7.22	8.31	9.15	9.73
October	6.34	8.57	7.68	8.38	9.72	9.19
November	6.66	7.31	7.90	8.17	10.34	8.68
December	6.50	7.56	8.23	8.56	10.85	8.50
Average	6.48	7.04	8.31	8.60	9.16	9.60

Fehr's "Review of the Oilseed and Oil Markets, 1925."

GENERAL PRICE DECLINE OF OILS AND OIL SEEDS, CONT'D

SOYA BEANS: Average monthly prices, C.I.F. Pacific Coast ports and
C.I.F. United Kingtom - Continent, March 1924 to March, 1926.
(Dollars per bushel of 60 pounds)

Month	C.I.F. Pacific Coast			C.I.F. U.K.-Continent		
	1924	1925	1926	1924	1925	1926
	Dollars	Dollars	Dollars	Dollars	Dollars	Dollars
January.......:		1.55	1.56 c/:		1.66	1.61 c/
February......:		1.53	1.59 b/:		1.58	1.61 b/
March.........:	1.42	1.51	1.57 d/:	1.45	1.55	1.60 d/
April.........:	1.35	1.59		1.42	1.62	
May...........:	1.38 a/	1.69 a/		1.42 a/:	1.76 a/	
June ....:	1.39	1.78		1.40	1.86	
July..........:	1.46	1.83		1.49	1.88	
August........:	1.58	1.95		1.64	1.98	
September.....:	1.58	1.87		1.65	1.83	
October......:	1.58	1.68 b/		1.73	1.77 b/	
November......:	1.54	1.56		1.66	1.66	
December......:	1.56	1.57 b/		1.68	1.65 b/	

Weekly reports of the Nisshin Oil Mills, Inc.,Dairen, Manchuria.
a/ Four weeks
b/ Three weeks
c/ Two weeks
d/ One week.

FLAXSEED: Average closing price per bushel, Minneapolis, average
1909-13, annual 1921 to 1926, for
No. 1 Flaxseed

Month	Year beginning September 1.					
	Average 1909-13	1921	1922	1923	1924	1925
	Cents	Cents	Cents	Cents	Cents	Cents
September.....:	195	203	228	238	226	259
October.......:	190	181	238	248	240	258
November......:	182	181	248	241	258	256
December......:	182	189	262	246	284	261
January.......:	194	213	280	250	315	250
February......:	196	246	304	258	312	243
March.........:	195	257	307	249	297	232
April.........:	198	270	340	247	279	234
May...........:	196	280	294	246	280	
June..........:	189	250	280	244	268	
July..........:	189	259	270	247	249	
August........:	196	229	234	244	254	
Average.......:	192	219	258	244	271	

Division of Statistical and Historical Research. Compiled from Annual Reports of
the Minneapolis Chamber of Commerce and Minneapolis Daily Market Record. From
January 1, 1921, average of daily prices are weighted by carlot sales. See also
Foreign Crops and Markets, Vol. 12, No. 11.

ESTIMATES OF UNITED STATES CONSUMPTION OF EDIBLE OILS

The following table gives estimates of the consumption in the United States for all purposes, the net factory consumption and other consumption, for the more important edible oils. In estimating the consumption for all purposes, the supply of each oil was calculated by adding together the stocks of oil in factories and warehouses at the beginning of the year, the total factory production of crude oil, and the imports less reexports of oil. From this total supply figure was subtracted the domestic exports and the stocks of oil at the end of the year. The resulting figure represents the quantity of oil going directly into trade channels or used for the manufacture of other products, and should not be confused with factory consumption.

Stocks, exports, and imports, of each oil, except olive, were reported for both crude and refined oil. To make all figures comparable the two were expressed in terms of crude oil by converting the refined to a crude basis, dividing the refined oil by the conversion factor given in the footnote. Cottonseed oil, for example, has an average refining loss of about 7 per cent. The conversion factor is therefore .93.

The stocks of oil used in these calculations include those in factories and warehouses, but not those in the hands of the smaller dealers. If the latter are subject to much variation from year to year some error may be expected in using these figures as a measure of final consumption.

The net factory consumption was obtained by adding the factory consumption of refined and crude oils and subtracting the factory production of refined, the refined oils being converted to a crude basis. The resulting figures do not, therefore, take into account the consumption of by-products of the refining process. No data are available as to how much of these products are recovered and used.

The net factory consumption of soybean oil in 1924 is larger than the estimated consumption for all purposes. This is probably due to inaccuracy in the statistics of distribution resulting from the fact that this oil is for the most part imported.

ESTIMATES OF UNITED STATES CONSUMPTION OF EDIBLE OILS, CONT'D.

VEGETABLE OILS: Estimated total disappearance in the
United States, 1921-1925 a/

Vegetable Oil	1921	1922	1923	1924	1925 (Preliminary)
	1,000 pounds	1,000 pounds	1,000 pounds	1,000 pounds	1,000 pounds
Cottonseed:					
Total disappearance..:	1,099,037:	965,878 :	890,881:	1,052,675 :	1,500,823
Net factory consumption...........:	982,969:	795,016 :	738,508:	866,170 :	1,267,307
Other consumption....:	116,068:	170,862 :	152,373:	186,505 :	233,516
Peanut:					
Total disappearance..:	46,440:	40,354 :	13,747:	9,854 :	19,941
Net factory consumption.........:	43,060:	34,154 :	9,204:	8,198 :	12,488
Other consumption....:	3,380:	6,200 :	4,543:	1,656 :	7,453
Soybean:					
Total disappearance..:	34,933:	20,829 :	37,583:	14,149 :	19,008
Net factory consumption..........:	34,004:	19,042 :	23,803:	15,094 :	17,192
Other consumption....:	929:	1,787 :	13,780: b/	(-)945 :	1,816
Olive, Edible:					
Total disappearance..:	50,830:	60,378 :	79,529:	79,486 :	87,490
Net factory consumption..........:	1,541:	3,093 :	1,584:	1,353 :	1,807
Other consumption....:	49,289:	57,285 :	77,945:	78,133 :	85,683
Coconut:					
Total disappearance..:	300,609:	382,078 :	439,357:	408,736 :	427,996
Net factory consumption..........:	252,902:	337,071 :	402,085:	403,324 :	398,707
Other consumption....:	47,707:	45,007 :	37,272:	5,412 :	29,289
Corn:					
Total disappearance..:	73,279:	115,089 :	108,868:	115,307 :	98,649
Net factory consumption..........:	14,198:	44,504 :	33,937:	28,211 :	27,732
Other consumption....:	59,081:	70,585 :	74,931:	87,096 :	70,917

a/ In terms of crude oil, except olive, which is expressed as edible.
Stocks, exports and imports of refined oil, except olive, converted to
a crude basis, using the factor .93 for cottonseed and corn oils and .94
for peanut, soybean, and coconut oils. In calculating net factory consumption, the factory production and consumption of refined oil was also
converted to a crude basis.
b/ Net factory consumption for the year is greater than estimated total
consumption.

ESTIMATES OF UNITED STATES CONSUMPTION OF EDIBLE OILS, CONT'D.

ANIMAL AND VEGETABLE FATS AND OILS: Factory Consumption in
the United States, 1921-1925.

Fat or oil	1921	1922	1923		
	1,000 pounds	1,000 pounds	1,000 pounds	1000 pounds	
Cottonseed, crude.......	1,295,740	895,162	934,995	1,163,821	1,469,00
Cottonseed, refined.....	895,033	734,069	675,246	779,858	1,151,31
Peanut, crude and virgin	42,543	28,372	7,504	8,651	10,26
Peanut, refined.........	34,686	28,907	7,548	5,684	10,44
Coconut or copra, crude.	235,090	305,330	360,002	363,770	386,36
Coconut or copra, refined....	139,418	165,080	211,940	210,901	209,63
Corn, crude.............	71,898	106,097	103,068	114,162	102,18
Corn, refined...........	7,766	28,288	18,596	13,987	10,39
Soybean, crude..........	28,822	17,570	19,341	10,749	11,32
Soybean, refined........	10,527	4,601	6,762	5,882	5,51
Olive, edible...........	2,515	3,678	2,158	2,862	2,33
Palm-kernel, crude......	2,658	1,923	4,530	5,362	50,99
Palm-kernel, refined....	1,839	194	398	206	4,417
Rapeseed................	7,445	10,159	11,439	12,200	11,495
Palm....................	22,827	43,962	114,385	78,656	109,954
Lard, neutral...........	29,490	29,345	31,230	29,770	26,119
Lard, other edible......	110,038	28,837	25,353	21,227	15,027
Tallow, edible..........	23,587	26,419	34,766	33,685	38,798
Lard compounds and other lard substitutes.	----	1,459	1,815	1,866	1,122
Oleo oil................	45,256	54,698	50,813	49,703	48,084
Animal stearin, edible..	42,918	52,023	49,590	55,094	59,323
Tallow oil..............	30,065	33,298	28,942	34,864	8,130
Lard oil................	9,105	14,709	20,429	18,860	21,531

Compiled from Reports of the Bureau of the Census.

The above figures of consumption cover consumption other than that used
for ordinary purposes, by households, retailers and bakeries, or by local
painters, contractors, etc. or for lubrication purposes of any kind.

ESTIMATES OF UNITED STATES CONSUMPTION OF EDIBLE OILS, CONT'D.

ANIMAL AND VEGETABLE FATS AND OILS: Factory Production in the United States,
fiscal year 1912-13 and calendar years, 1921-1925.

Fat or oil	Year end- ing June 30, 1913 a/	1921	1922	1923	1924	1925 (Prel.)
	1,000 pounds	1,000 pounds	1,000 pounds	1,000 pounds	1,000 pounds	1,000 pounds
Cottonseed, crude........	1,455,401	1,277,300	934,627	973,753	1,154,434	1,506,088
Cottonseed, refined.....	....	1,185,910	827,205	857,979	1,056,673	1,338,887
Peanut, crude & virgin..	454	33,234	22,644	5,359	6,691	15,852
Peanut, refined.........	-....	34,200	23,472	5,950	6,110	8,360
Coconut or copra, crude..	31,729	113,194	185,526	235,919	191,357	207,604
Coconut or copra, re- fined..............		122,675	135,243	172,382	173,720	198,030
Corn, crude.............	73,833	87,481	111,508	111,343	117,065	104,157
Corn, refined...........	.....	61,427	85,569	82,888	93,922	79,633
Soya-bean, crude........	.....	.....	751	1,404	950	1,406
Soya-bean, refined......	.....	5,656	3,218	2,568	1,797	----
Olive, edible...........	966	974	585	574	1,509	532
Palm-kernel, crude......	3,200	1,327	.....	.....	----	----
Palm-kernel, refined....	.....	979	800	690	632	1,032
Rapeseed................	90	128	58	.....	30	----
Lard, neutral...........	....	63,110	49,432	60,961	68,324	46,629
Lard, other edible......		1,454,855	1,575,640	1,944,862	1,934,545	1,499,484
Tallow, edible..........		41,238	49,108	52,923	51,676	50,219
Lard compounds & other.. lard substitutes.....	.....	......	784,180	750,522	830,435	1,137,973
Oleo oil................	.....	147,683	164,780	158,610	156,334	141,166
Animal stearin, edible..	.....	70,644	75,295	71,942	78,370	73,956
Tallow oil..............	.....	10,512	11,975	36,271	30,435	11,859
Lard oil................	.....	16,724	26,034	34,278	29,169	35,450
Oleomargarine b/........	145,228	190,950	209,182	239,699	215,403	----

Compiled from reports of the Bureau of the Census, except 1913.
a/ Bureau of Chemistry.
b/ Annual report of the Commissioner of Internal Revenue, year beginning July 1.

The above figures of production include all production other than that of
lard, tallow and grease in the households, on the farms and by the small local
butchers and meat markets.

ESTIMATES OF UNITED STATES CONSUMPTION OF EDIBLE OILS, CONT'D

ANIMAL AND VEGETABLE FATS AND OILS: Stocks in the United
States, December 31, 1920-1925 a/

Fat or oil	1920	1921	1922	1923	1924	1925 (Prel.)
	1,000 pounds	1,000 pounds	1,000 pounds	1,000 pounds	1,000 pounds	1,000 pounds
Cottonseed, crude......:	156,089:	99,669:	109,444:	141,027:	105,992:	119,124
Cottonseed, refined....:	274,389:	258,351:	147,129:	147,187:	232,390:	167,028
Peanut, crude and virgin:	21,989:	12,381:	1,661:	1,296:	1,531:	1,545
Peanut, refined........:	8,699:	6,148:	956:	672:	2,324:	993
Coconut or copra, crude:	84,009:	78,896:	94,031:	49,853:	51,980:	46,339
Coconut or copra, re- fined............:	28,187:	25,662:	25,532:	27,277:	12,729:	11,469
Corn, crude...........:	5,537:	9,723:	6,186:	7,082:	7,932:	7,951
Corn, refined.........:	11,621:	16,844:	11,472:	8,884:	6,307:	7,831
Soybean, crude........:	22,858:	9,452:	3,606:	7,845:	2,012:	1,728
Soybean, refined......:	7,883:	1,587:	1,761:	1,510:	775:	688
Olive, edible.........:	6,884:	6,542:	7,869:	6,034:	4,131:	7,257
Palm-kernel, crude.....:	1,596:	282:	1,056:	1,144:	1,426:	9,014
Palm-kernel, refined...:	29:	214:	435:	71:	97:	303
Rapeseed..............:	3,901:	1,793:	2,038:	3,300:	3,956:	3,083
Palm ....:	4,688:	4,598:	15,766:	18,753:	23,648:	25,838
Lard, neutral.........:	4,700:	5,351:	4,995:	3,747:	6,438:	2,590
Lard, other edible.....:	59,808:	44,573:	42,923:	44,609:	56,097:	42,974
Tallow, edible........:	5,197:	5,175:	3,292:	3,681:	3,360:	3,855
Lard, compound and other: lard substitutes...:	.....:	.....:	15,515:	10,689:	19,517:	22,857
Oleo oil..............:	17,169:	11,801:	11,949:	9,804:	15,481:	10,348
Animal stearin, edible :	7,347:	5,173:	5,806:	6,287:	7,503:	5,762
Tallow oil............:	5,901:	3,033:	2,637:	3,398:	2,680:	1,889
Lard oil..............:	4,394:	3,273:	3,898:	5,142:	4,396:	4,837

Compiled from reports of the Bureau of the Census.
a/ Stocks in factories and warehouses.

The above figures of stocks include all stocks other than those in the hands of households, local tradesmen, retailers, wholesalers or jobbers except such as may be held in public warehouses. Stocks in the hands of importers and exporters are included.

ESTIMATES OF UNITED STATES CONSUMPTION OF EDIBLE OILS, CONT'D

OLEOMARGARINE: Materials used in its Manufacture in the
United States for the years ending June 30, 1921
to 1925.

Materials	1921	1922	1923	1924	1925
	Pounds	Pounds	Pounds	Pounds	Pounds
Oleo oil ....:	49,675,749:	40,979,979:	46,644,830:	52,264,573:	44,102,320
Coconut oil.......:	103,111,916:	57,393,661:	65,656,312:	83,059,335:	79,449,432
Cottonseed oil....:	18,532,860:	15,420,018:	18,757,074:	20,640,341:	20,965,709
Peanut oil.......:	16,332,498:	11,624,846:	6,921,796:	5,656,488:	4,391,937
Oleo stearin......:	4,857,972:	4,574,070:	4,815,089:	5,316,728:	5,249,676
Neutral lard......:	29,267,960:	27,057,263:	29,567,577:	32,210,041:	25,673,625
Oleo stock........:	2,065,231:	2,142,720:	2,322,042:	2,755,798:	3,182,657
Butter...........:	1,498,625:	1,107,416:	1,575,566:	1,900,307:	1,509,063
Milk.............:	79,715,584:	53,938,989:	59,835,266:	69,089,727:	61,923,973
Mustard seed oil..:	109,748:			38,243:	27,181
Palm kernel oil...:	:	:	:	26,432: a/	346,904
Edible tallow.....:	233,227:	:	:	23,575:	110,875
Sesamum oil.......:	:	:	:	347,719:	268,381
Corn oil.........:	925,999:	:	:	457,170:	196,332
Soybean oil......:	461,129:	:	:	49:	- - - -
Vegetable oil.....:	6,559,034:	:	:	:	
Salt.............:	25,365,499:	16,261,850:	17,998,321:	20,592,762:	18,724,864
Sugar............:	:	:	:	280:	- - - -
Soda.............:	:	:	:	57,466:	57,994
Extract of vanilla:	:	:	:	97:	334
Coloring.........:	25,915:	11,056:	11,385:	26,116:	38,155
Miscellaneous.....:	3,216,742:	3,417,241:	2,917,566:	- - - -	14,367
Total.........:	341,955,688:	233,929,109:	257,022,824:	294,463,247:	266,233,779

Annual Reports of Commissioner of Internal Revenue.

a/ Stated as palm oil.

ANIMAL AND VEGETABLE FATS AND OILS: Foreign trade of the United States, 1913, 1921-1925

	: Year ending:	Year ending December 31		
	: June 30, :	:	:	:
Fat or oil	: 1913 :	1923 :	1924 :	1925
	: 1,000 :	1,000 :	1,000 :	1,000 ·
NET IMPORTS: a/	: pounds :	pounds :	pounds :	pounds
Peanut.........................:	8,956 :	7,721 :	5,155:	2,687
Coconut.......................:	50,386 :	161,116 :	204,029:	213,411
Soy bean......................:	12,149 :	40,151 :	6,584:	17,226
Olive, edible ....:	39,109 :	77,120 :	76,074:	90,084
Palm kernel...................::	(23,536 :	(126,799 :	(104,880:	(188,217
Palm..........................::	(50,169 :	(:	(:	(
Cocoa butter..................::	3,483 :	c/ :	914:	c/
Rape seed.....................:d/	11,623 :d/	15,932 :	17,362:	12,735
Tallow, vegetable.............::	0 :d/	8,548 :d/	5,197:	6,424
Beef and hog fats.............:	0 :d/	11,374 :d/	3,537:	2,724
	:	:	:	:
NET EXPORTS: b/	:	:	:	:
Vegetable oil lard compound....:	0 :	9,617 :	6,989:	8,223
Cottonseed, crude and refined..:	311,917 :	49,583 :	43,343:	62,415
Corn..........................:	19,839 :	4,361 :	3,679:	3,847
Lard..........................:	519,025 :1,035,382 :	944,095:	688,829
Lard, neutral.................:	44,778 :	24,129 :	27,365:	18,854
Lard compounds................:	67,457 :	7,451 :	7,382:	14,091
Tallow, edible................:	30,586 :	1,204 :	989: e/	17,514
Oleo oil......................:	92,850 :	98,955 :	99,380:	91,791
Lard oil......................:	155 :	736 :	475: f/	
Oleomargarine, animal.........:	2,968 :	1,792 :	774:	627
" vegetable.......:	0 :	1,745 :	127:	148
Cocoa butter..................:g/	:	361 :g/	:	2,401
Stearin and fatty acids –	:	:	:	
Oleo stearin.............:f/	:	(:	(:	(
Lard stearin, edible.......:f/	:	(8,765 :	(6,575:	7,395
Grease stearin.............:f/	:	3,520 :	3,008:	2,631
Oleic acid or red oil......:f/	:	1,737 :	2,689:	491
Stearins and other fatty acids :f/	:	2,863 :	2,198:h/	1,929

Compiled from Foreign Commerce and Navigation of the United States, 1913, 1921
    1924, and Monthly Summary of Foreign Commerce of the United States,
    December, 1925.
a/ Net imports equal general imports minus domestic exports, minus re exports.
b/ Net exports equal domestic exports plus re-exports, minus general imports.
c/ Net exports.
d/ Imports only, reexports not separately classified.
e/ Includes "Inedible tallow."   f/ Not separately classified. g/ Net imports.
h/ Excludes "Other fatty acids."

VEGETABLE OILS AND OIL MATERIAL: Imports into the United States, by countries, 1913, 1923-1925

Country from which imported	Year ending June 30, 1913	Year ending December 31		
		1923	1924	1925
PEANUTS, SHELLED	Short tons	Short tons	Short tons	Short tons
Japan	571	5,743	1,234	28
Spain	1,296	322	729	53
France	662	0	0	0
China	223	17,226	24,853	36,023
Hongkong	51	62	32	16
Java and Madura	a/	587	783	152
Other countries	593	242	357	295
Total imports	3,401	24,182	27,988	36,567
PEANUTS, UNSHELLED				
Japan	4,125	519	223	768
Spain	1,739	135	22	91
China	176	1,272	2,204	4,145
Hongkong	38	32	24	27
Other countries	63	11	3	199
Total imports	6,141	1,969	2,476	5,228
COPRA				
Philippine Islands	11,764	129,948	119,289	142,030
French Oceania	3,343	13,574	11,183	11,196
British Oceania	995	9,866	6,574	5,156
Australia	1	6,633	187	5,604
Other countries	1,031	6,466	8,299	18,052
Total imports	17,134	166,487	145,532	182,038
PEANUT OIL	1,000 pounds	1,000 pounds	1,000 pounds	1,000 pounds
France	3,958	1,002	1,069	729
Germany	2,496	5	0	55
Netherlands	1,801	302	56	86
Hongkong	512	1,645	1,742	1,504
China	83	3,176	11,941	572
England	43	1,241	10	0
Other countries	70	638	577	81
Total imports	8,968	8,009	15,395	3,027
Olive Oil, EDIBLE				
Italy	26,887	49,722	53,236	61,984
France	5,994	5,638	5,856	7,500
Spain	3,623	18,703	14,039	15,537
Other countries	2,654	2,077	3,055	5,385
Total imports	39,158	77,190	76,186	90,426

Compiled from Foreign Commerce and Navigation of the United States, and official records of the Bureau of Foreign and Domestic Commerce.
a/ If any, included in "Dutch East Indies."

continued-

VEGETABLE OILS AND OIL MATERIAL: Imports into the United States, by countries, 1913, 1923-1925, cont'd.

Country from which imported	:Year ending: June 30, 1913	Year ending December 31		
		1923	1924	1925
	1,000 pounds	1,000 pounds	1,000 pounds	1,000 pounds
PALM OIL				
United Kingdom.............:	38,795	43,311	19,769	31,445
Germany....................:	11,301	10,603	20,452	11,959
British West Africa........:	0	54,253	42,194	5,840
Belgian Congo..............:	0	10,226	13,935	21,217
Netherlands................:	0	5,322	2,538	3,966
Other countries............:	133	4,770	8,892	64,752
Total imports..........:	50,229	128,495	101,780	139,179
PALM KERNEL OIL				
United Kingdom.............:	3,788 a/		4,318	47,526
Germany....................:	18,831 a/		119	4,728
Other countries............:	950 a/		311	370
Total imports..........:	23,569 a/		4,748	52,624
SOYBEAN OIL				
Japan......................:	7,979	466	1	180
China......................:	1,172	1,250	1,501	3,431
Kwantung, leased territory.............:	108	39,787	6,496	15,587
Other countries............:	3,081	176	1,127	295
Total imports..........:	12,340	41,679	9,125	19,493
COCONUT OIL				
United Kingdom.............:	12,665	35	34	289
British India..............:	3,313	1,033	92	101
Other Br. E. Indies, including Ceylon........:	22,768	113	0	0
Philippine Islands.........:	1,384	180,700	224,635	232,499
Other countries............:	10,374	1	2	285
Total imports..........:	50,504	181,982	224,763	233,174
CASTOR BEANS	Short tons	Short tons	Short tons	Short tons
British India..............:	20,843	40,283	35,678	42,189
Brazil.....................:	224	3,921	3,634	9,878
Other countries............:	1,127	66	3,177	1,549
Total imports..........:	22,194	44,270	42,489	53,616

Compiled from Foreign Commerce and Navigation of the United States and official reports of the Bureau of Foreign and Domestic Commerce.
a/ Not separately classified.

Continued –

VEGETABLE OILS AND OIL MATERIALS: Imports into the United States, by countries, 1913, 1923-1925, cont'd

Country from which imported	:Year ending : June 30, 1913	Year ending December 31		
		1923	1924	1925
	1,000 pounds	1,000 pounds	1,000 pounds	1,000 pounds
RAPE OIL				
United Kingdom ....:	9,933	14,698	16,101	1,186
Other countries..........:	1,690	1,234	1,261	512
Total.............:	11,623	15,932	17,362	1,698
COCOA BUTTER				
Netherlands..............:	2,705	71	735	48
Germany........~.........:	860	343	1,016	2
Other countries..........:	38	4	28	14
Total ....:	3,603	418	1,779	64
POPPY SEED	Short tons	Short tons	Short tons	Short tons
Netherlands...........:a/		2,921	2,409	:a/
Germany...............:a/		209	26	:a/
Other countries........:a/		144	297	:a/
Total...........:a/		3,274	2,732	:a/

Compiled from Foreign Commerce and Navigation of the United States and official reports of the Bureau of Foreign and Domestic Commerce.
a/ Not separately classified.

- - - - - - -

VEGETABLE OILS AND OIL MATERIAL: Exports from the United States, by countries, 1913, 1923-1925

Country to which exported	Year ending: June 30, 1913	Year ending December 31		
		1923	1924	1925
	Short tons	Short tons	Short tons	Short tons
PEANUTS				
Canada...................:	2,684	2,013	1,308	1,555
United Kingdom...........:	316	1	3	14
Guiana (British, Dutch and French)...........:	272	59	5	2
Cuba.....................:	54	61	34	35
Jamaica..................:	51	47	29	10
Panama...................:	49	53	26	32
Mexico...................:	44	15	17	14
Other countries..........:	181	154	141	82
Total................:	3,651	2,403	1,563	1,744
	1,000 pounds	1,000 pounds	1,000 pounds	1,000 pounds
COCONUT OIL				
Canada...................:a/		10,413	8,632	7,767
Mexico...................:a/		3,980	7,135	7,994
Cuba.....................:a/		1,669	1,409	1,083
Other countries..........:a/		500	784	1,057
Total ....:a/		16,562	17,960	17,901

Continued —

VEGETABLE OILS AND OIL MATERIAL: Exports from the United States by countries, 1913, 1923-1925, cont'd

Country to which exported	Year ending: June 30, 1913	Year ending December 31		
		1923	1924	1925
	1,000 pounds	1,000 pounds	1,000 pounds	1,000 pounds
COTTONSEED OIL, refined				
Netherlands............:	76,922	106	6,744	4,895
Italy ....:	39,517	6	10	20
United Kingdom ....:	31,845	21	199	758
Canada.................:	25,227	1,070	1,053	1,256
Mexico ....:	23,744	5,201	4,028	2,956
France ....:	17,924	368	106	670
Argentina ....:	14,708	1,240	0	2,055
Norway ....:	8,986	2,399	1,279	2,578
Cuba ....:	4,830	2,532	955	5,567
Chile ....:	3,639	2,177	478	569
Uruguay ....:	3,530	1,311	152	88
Other countries ....:	64,361	5,395	9,390	7,450
Total ....:	315,233	21,826	24,394	28,862
COTTONSEED OIL, crude				
Canada ....:b/		24,722	17,126	31,728
Mexico ....:b/		3,030	1,703	1,739
Argentina ....:b/		0 :c/		32
Other countries ....:b/		30	119	55
Total ....:b/		27,782	18,948	33,554
PEANUT OIL				
Norway ....:a/		0	0 :a/	
Canada ....:a/		188	13 :a/	
Cuba ....:a/		0	3 :a/	
Denmark ....:a/		0	0 :a/	
Mexico ....:a/		3 :c/	:a/	
Japan ....:a/		0 :c/	:a/	
New Zealand ....:a/		6	0 :a/	
Australia ....:a/	:c/		21 :a/	
Other countries ....:a/		6	1 :a/	
Total ....:a/		203	38 :a/	
SOYBEAN OIL				
Netherlands ....:a/		0	0	0
Canada ....:a/		208	115	413
Italy ....:a/		0	0	0
Yugoslavia & Albania ..:a/		19	0	0
Jamaica ....:a/		409	338	23
Cuba ....:a/		106	503	1
Chile ....:a/		277	83	0
Uruguay ....:a/		278	1,121	67
Other countries ....:a/		59	104	16
Total ....:a/		1,356	2,264	520

a/ Not separately classified. b/ Included in "Refined". c/ Less than 500 pounds.

Continued -

VEGETABLE OILS AND-OIL MATERIAL: Exports from the United States,
by countries, 1913, 1923-1925, cont'd

Country to which exported	Year ending: June 30, 1913	Year ending December 31		
		1923	1924	1925
	1,000 pounds	1,000 pounds	1,000 pounds	1,000 pounds
CORN OIL				
Italy	6,259	0	00	0
Belgium	2,953	0	0	0
Germany	2,356 a/		6	19
Sweden	2,302	0	0	0
Canada	1,199	157	138	234
Netherlands	781	0 a/		0
British So. Africa	28	768	1,308	1,216
Dominican Republic	18	873	611	489
Cuba	a/	1,020	939	929
Greece	0	19	0	0
Panama	0	14	38	62
Jamaica	0	403	34	14
Chile	0	129	0	0
Other countries	3,943	978	605	884
Total	19,839	4,361	3,679	3,847
COCOA BUTTER				
Canada	b/	463	520	2,192
Japan	b/	236	251	61
Cuba	b/	12	12	54
China	b/	19	15	29
Other countries	b/	32	48	96
Total	b/	762	846	2,432
VEGETABLE OLEOMARGARINE				
Canada	b/	299	3 a/	
Germany	b/	25	0	0
United Kingdom	b/	1	0	2
Panama	b/	26	15	18
Japan	b/	21	60	12
Ukraine	b/	1,305	0	0
Other countries	b/	69	49	116
Total	b/	1,745	127	148

Compiled from Foreign Commerce and Navigation of the United States and official
reports of the Bureau of Foreign and Domestic Commerce.

a/ Less than 500 pounds.
b/ Not separately classified.

PEANUTS: International trade, average 1911-1913, annual 1924-1925

Country	Average 1911-1913		1924		1925 preliminary	
	Imports	Exports	Imports	Exports	Imports	Exports
Principal exporting countries	1,000 pounds	1,000 pounds	1,000 pounds	1,000 pounds	1,000 pounds	1,000 pounds
Anglo-Egyptian Sudan:	--:	1,961:	--:	22,987:	--:	--
Brazil:	--:	274:	--:	--:	--:	--
British India:	--:	503,448:	--:	550,505:	--:	1,036,670
China:	32,882:	138,472:	22,921:	661,267:	--:	--
Dutch East Indies:	612:	60,282:	511:	43,099:	--:	--
Mozambique:	a/ 1,098:	a/ 15,907:	--:	--:	--:	--
French Possessions in India:	--:	306,701:	--:	--:	--:	--
Nigeria:	--:	17,163:	--:	--:	--:	--
Senegal:	a/ 168:	425,937:	--:	--:	--:	--
Spain:	--:	9,205:	--:b/	3,764:	--:	--
Tanganyika:	--:c/	9,275:	--:	9,056:	--:	--
Principal importing countries						
Algeria:	7,022:	218:	7,906:	259:	--:	348
Argentina:	8,667:	--:	554:	2,883:b/	1,853:b/	55
British Malaya:	c/ 19,488:	c/d/ 10839:	14,941:	2,006:	--:	--
Canada:	7,302:	--:	22,283:	--:	23,793:	--
Denmark:	5,236:	--:	20,178:	--:	27,290:	--
Egypt:	4,664:	1,637:	7,406:	4,504:	13,863:	3,925
France:	1,239,659:	47,107:	1,359,166:	17,760:	1,503,923:	16,082
Germany:	174,970:c/	98:	165,178:	--:	713,245:	--
Hongkong:	--:	--:	60,265:	41,277:	--:	42
Italy...f/:	1,194:	804:	57,859:	48:	97,271:	42
Japan:	--:	10,675:	32,147:	401:g/	10,973:g/	1,957
Netherlands:	122,862:	32,863:	148,528:	4,877:	229,545:	2,004
Philippine Islands:	2,264:	--:	3 058:	--:	--:	--
Tunis:	e/ 1,459:	--:	3,369:	--:	--:	--
Union of South Africa:	3,164:	7:	1,264:	29:	--:	--
United Kingdom:	--:	--:	226,216:	--:	277,583:	--
United States:	20,988:	6,804:	88,913:	3,127:	120,158:	3,499
Other countries:	100,697:	248,180:	9,184:	958:	32,839:	438
Total:	1,754,396:	1,847,857:	2,251,849:	1,368,807:	3,052,336:	1,055,020

Compiled from official sources except where otherwise noted.
Includes shelled and unshelled, assuming the peanuts to be unshelled unless otherwise stated. When shelled nuts were reported they have been reduced to terms of unshelled at the ratio of three pounds unshelled to two pounds shelled.

a/ Two-year average. b/ Six months. c/ International Institute of Agriculture, Oleaginous Products and Vegetable Oils. d/ Three-year average. e/ One year only. f/ Reports include some sesamum. g/ Five months.

OLIVE OIL(INCLUDING INEDIBLE): International trade, average 1909-1913,
annual 1924-1925

Country	Year ending December 31					
	a/ Average 1909-1913		1924		1925 preliminary	
	Imports	Exports	Imports	Exports	Exports	Imports
	1.000 pounds	1,000 pounds	1,000 pounds	1,000 pounds	1,000 pounds	1,000 pounds
PRINCIPAL EXPORTING COUNTRIES						
Algeria...............:b/	974:b/	11,566:	167:	28,354:	153:	25,354
Greece................:	--:	22,272:	165:	19,649:	--:	--
Italy...............:b/	6,643:	73,130:	335:	93,780:	644:	94,901
Spain.................:	31:	86,454:	1:	101,695:c/ 1/	:c/	4,049
Tunis.................:	2,030:	18,030:	4,267:	19,638:	--:	--
Yugoslavia e/.........:	--:	--:	860:	1,210:	:	
PRINCIPAL IMPORTING COUNTRIES						
Argentina.............:	48,248:	--:e/	64,639:	--:	--:	--
Australia.............:	510:	11:a/f/	1,053:d/f/	:	--:	--
Belgium..............:b/	4,295:b/	583:	2,076:	53:	1,829:	51
Brazil................:	8,400:	--:	--:	--:	--:	--
Bulgaria..............:	4,003:	7:	2,048:	--:	--:	--
Canada................:	1,593:	--:	2,528:	--:	2,378:	--
Chile.................:	7,255:	--:	--:	--:	--:	--
Cuba..................:	--:	--:	16,035:	--:	--:	--
Denmark...............:	146:	--:	135:	10:	--:	--
Egypt.................:	4,803:	--:	3,043:	23:	3,344:	34
France...............:b/	42,502:	12,935:	38,459:	12,759:	41,152:	9,905
Germany...............:	6,095:	--:	2,000:	44:	3,352:	35
Japan.................:	123:	--:	227:	--:g/	181:	--
Macao (Portuguese China) e/:	--:	--:	4,752:	4,479:	--:	--
Morocco...............:	267:	375:	300:	5,623:	--:	--
Netherlands..........:b/	283:b/	205:	174:	22:	190:	9
New Zealand...........:	68:	--:	136:	--:	--:	--
Norway................:	3,458:	33:	9,978:	--:	4,717:	--
Peru.................:b/	694:b/	77:	901:d/	--:	--:	--
Philippine Islands....:	360:	--:	276:	--:	--:	--
Portugal.............:b/	2,020:b/	5,492:	1,240:	2,609:	--:	--
Rumania...............:	7,338:	--:	1,549:	1:b/	1,566:d/h/	--
Sweden................:	883:	2:	400:d/	:	--:	--
Switzerland...........:	4,130:	71:	3,295:e/	36:	3,542:d/	
United Kingdom........:	22,950:	823:	18,872:	302:	17,244:	311
United States........:	39,903:	--:	109,104:	--:	142,133:	--
Uruguay...............:	4,249:	--:	10,640:	--:	12,739:	--
Other countries.......:	40,445:	24,633:	11,657:	708:	2,226:d/	
Total.............:	264,683:	258,758:	310,252:	291,351:	237,400:	134,549

Compiled from official sources except where otherwise noted. Conversions made on the basis of 7.5 pounds to the gallon.
/ International Institute of Agriculture, Oleaginous Products and Vegetable Oils.
/ Four-year average. c/ Six months. d/ Less than 500 pounds. e/ International Yearbook of Agricultural Statistics. f/ Year beginning July 1. g/ Five months.
/ Nine months.

COTTONSEED OIL: International trade, average 1909-1913, annual 1924-1925

Country	Average 1909-1913		1924		1925 preliminary	
	Imports	Exports	Imports	Exports	Imports	Exports
Principal exporting countries	1,000 pounds	1,000 pounds	1,000 pounds	1,000 pounds	1,000 pounds	1,000 pounds
Brazil	4,680;a/	12:	--:	--:	--:	
China	--:	2,110:	--:	1,374:	3.91:	8,101
Egypt	1,927:	3,568:	34:	16,085:	391:	
Peru	--:b/c/	158:	--:	10,083:	--:	--
United Kingdom	44,246:	53,920:	16,524:	50,180:	11,294:	44,139
United States	d/ 4,715:	292,257:	--:	43,343:	:	62,415
Principal importing countries						
Algeria	2,728:	1,177:	85:	17:	--:	--
Argentina	7,510:	12:	517:	--:e/	857:	--
Australia	1,062:	--:	--:	--:	:	--
Belgium	16,884:	8,143:	2,094:f/	:	2,689:	--
Canada	21,131:	--:	20,495:	--:	30,136:	--
Czechoslovakia	--:	--:	1,214:	:	233:	--
Denmark	c/ 7,081:	--:	3,466:	1,180:	4,732:	--
France	24,666:	2,509:	7,225:	92:	8,596:	38
Germany	51,884:	--:	14,204:	--:	30,652:	38
Greece	--:	--:	1,735:	--:	:	--
Italy	34,498:	6:	36:f/	:	105:	2
Mexico	27,052:g/	2,559:	--:	--:	--:	--
Netherlands	40,141:	392:	21,162:	5,604:	22,643:	5,015
Norway	11,284:	--:	5,552:	--:	5,102:	--
Sweden	5,220:d/	20:	1,555:	--:	--:	--
Uruguay	b/ 3,938:	--:	133:	--:	146:	--
Other countries	27,023:	282:	4,599:	225:	647:	2,107
Total	337,670:	367,125:	100,630:	128,183:	118,223:	119,855

Compiled from official sources except where otherwise noted.
a/ One year only. b/ International Institute of Agriculture. c/ Four-year averag
d/ Three-year average. e/ Six months. f/ Less than 500 pounds. g/ Two-year average.

CHINESE WOOD OIL: Total exports from China and imports into the
United States, 1922 to 1925

Year	:	Exports from China	:	Imports into the United States. a/
	:	Pounds	:	Pounds
1922	:	99,408,669	:	79,089,292
1923	:	111,584,953	:	87,291,675
1924	:	119,471,733	:	81,587,854
1925	:		:	101,553,519

Reports of the Chinese Maritime Customs, and Summary of Trade and Navigation of
the United States.

a/, Gallons reduced to pounds on the basis of 1 gallon = 7½ pounds.

PEANUT OIL: International trade, average 1909-1913, annual
1924 and 1925

Country	: a/	Average 1909-1913		1924		1925 preliminary	
		Imports	Exports	Imports	Exports	Imports	Exports
Principal exporting countries	:	1,000 pounds	1,000 pounds	1,000 pounds	1,000 pounds	1,000 pounds	1,000 pounds
Belgium	:	2,233	3,065:	3,598:	4,945:	9,187:	5,030
China	:b/		:c/ 35,593:b/	:	89,636:	---:	---
France	:	142	50,967:	3,154:	66,384:	3,815:	58,416
Netherlands	:	2,743	18,569:	19,134:	24,281:	40,210:	26,336
United Kingdom	:b/	:b/	:	10,980:	21,784:	---:	---
Principal importing countries	:						
Algeria	:b/	:b/	:	30,248:	539:	---:	---
Canada	:	---	---:	26,424:	---:	16,134:	---
Denmark	:	2,941	:c/ 156:	828:	2,019:	1,890:	---
Germany	:	1,602	---:	13,792:	6,141:	23,016:	12,967
Hongkong	:	---	---:	41,142:	27,691:	---:	---
Italy	:	8,867	:c/ 4:	8,605:	3:	9,168:	105
Morocco	:b/	:	---:	2,448:	---:	---:	---
Norway	:b/	:b/	:	7,261:	---:	8,449:	---
Philippine Islands	:c/	976	:b/	3,754:b/	:	---:	---
Sweden	:	2,459	---:	6,251:	333:	---:	---
United States	:d/	7,295	:b/	15,395:	39:	3,027:	---
Other countries	:	6,466	458:	1,233:	484:	1,543:	1,549
Total	:	35,724	107,812:	194,247:	244,279:	116,439:	104,403

Compiled from official sources except where otherwise noted.
Conversions made on the basis of 7.5 pounds to the gallon.
a/ International Institute of Agriculture, Oleaginous Products and Vegetable Oils.
b/ Not separately stated.   c/ Four-year average.   d/ Three-year average.

GRAINS: Exports from the United States, July 1-May 8, 1924-25 and 1925-26
PORK: Exports from the United States, July 1-May 8, 1924-25 and 1925-26

Commodity	July 1-May 8		Week ending			
	1924-25	1925-26 a/	April 17: 1926	April 24: 1926	May 1 1926	May 8 1926
GRAINS:	1,000	1,000	1,000	1,000	1,000	1,000
	Bushels	Bushels	Bushels:	Bushels:	Bushels:	Bushels
Wheat...............	180,079	45,935	220	582	315	950
Wheat flour b/c/ .	58,994	38,676	776	658	992	630
Rye................	44,910	47,877	167	296	249	263
Corn...............	6,934	19,705	372	328	183	317
Oats...............	6,040	25,409	431	389	401	311
Barley.............	18,822	25,117	309	127	310	585
PORK:	1,000	1,000	1,000	1,000	1,000	1,000
	pounds	pounds	pounds	pounds	pounds	pounds
Hams and shoulders,						
inc. Wiltshire sides:	249,719	179,390	1,824	1,696	2,097	2,080
Bacon, including						
Cumberland sides..	217,923	169,169	4,324	2,514	4,406	3,832
Lard	683,226	571,334	12,904	7,881	12,763	11,573
Pickled pork.......	23,241	23,399	320	106	350	384

Compiled from official records of the Bureau of Foreign and Domestic Commerce.
a/ Revised to March 31, 1926, including exports from all ports. b/ In terms of
bushels of wheat. c/ Includes flour milled in bond from Canadian wheat.

- - - - - -

GERMANY: Slaughtering at 36 most important slaughter points, first
          three months 1925 and 1926

Classification	First 3 months 1925	First 3 months 1926
Cattle	196,161	198,237
Calves	294,812	316,405
Total cattle and calves	490,973	514,642
Sheep	241,367	218,902
Hogs	763,653	837,940

Deutscher Reichsanzeiger, April 13, 1926.

BUTTER: Prices in London, Berlin, Copenhagen and New York.
(By Weekly Cable)

Market and Item	May 7, 1926	May 14, 1926	May 15, 1925
New York, 92 score a/ ....:	40.00	41.50	44.00
Copenhagen, official quotation :	34.60	37.00	37.00
Berlin, 1a quality a/ ....:	39.55	35.22	b/
London:			
Danish....................:	c/	c/	39.22
Dutch, unsalted...........:	c/	c/	38.78
New Zealand...............:	c/	c/	36.83
New Zealand, unsalted.....:	c/	c/	38.57
Australian................:	c/	c/	35.10
Australian, unsalted......:	c/	c/	35.97
Argentine, unsalted.......:	c/	c/	33.15
Siberian..................:	c/	c/	32.28

Quotations converted at exchange of the day. a/ Thursday price. b/ Not
received at that time. c/ No quotations during British strike. Prices
fixed at maximum quotations as of April 30, 1926.

EUROPEAN LIVESTOCK AND MEAT MARKETS
(By Weekly Cable)

Market and Item	Unit	Week ending		
		May 5, 1926	May 12, 1926	May 13, 1925
GERMANY:				
Receipts of hogs, 14 markets ... :	Number	49,468	52,477	50,955
Prices of hogs, Berlin ....:	$ per 100 lbs.:	15.64	16.32	13.45
Prices of lard, tcs. Hamburg....:	"	16.85	17.37	17.99
UNITED KINGDOM AND IRELAND:				
Hogs, certain markets, England	Number	c/	c/	11,503
Hogs, purchases, Ireland........:	"	c/	c/	
Prices at Liverpool:				
American Wiltshires...........:	$ per 100 lbs.:	c/	c/	19.92
Canadian " ....:	"	c/	c/	21.65
Danish " ....:	"	c/	c/	25.77
Imports, Great Britain: a/b/				
Mutton, frozen ....:	Carcasses	76,828		
Lamb, " ....:	"	101,094		
Beef, " ....:	Quarters	10,486		
Beef, chilled ....:	"	135,669		
DENMARK:				
Exports, of bacon a/ ....:	1,000 lbs.	7,949	5,130	

a/ Received through the Department of Commerce. b/ Week ending Tuesday preceding date indicated. c/ No data during British strike. Prices fixed at maximum
quotations as of April 30, 1926.

Index